Before beginning *The 8-Week Cholesterol Cure* program or any other medical or nutritional regimen, consult your physician to be sure it is appropriate for you.

The information in this book reflects the author's experiences and is not intended to replace medical advice. Any questions on symptoms, general or specific, should be addressed to your physician.

The 8-Week Cholesterol Cure Personal Diary

Robert E. Kowalski

Produced in association with

Cader Books

1817

Harper & Row Publishers, New York
Grand Rapids, Philadelphia, St. Louis, San Francisco
London, Singapore, Sydney, Tokyo, Toronto

Cader Company, Inc.
23 West 9th Street
New York, N.Y. 10011

FIRST EDITION
LIBRARY OF CONGRESS CATALOGUE CARD NUMBER 89-4583
ISBN 0-06-096471-5

89 90 91 92 93 HC 10 9 8 7 6 5 4 3 2 1

How to Use This Diary

The program outlined in detail in *The 8-Week Cholesterol Cure* is designed—and proven—to lower cholesterol levels by 20, 30, even 40 percent or more. That's because this is the only program to consider all three reasons for elevated cholesterol. You've been eating too much fat and cholesterol, so I show you some delicious ways to cut back on those culprits. Your body doesn't excrete sufficient cholesterol in the form of bile salts and bile acids through your intestine, so eating oat bran will increase the amount of cholesterol excreted. And your liver has been producing too much cholesterol, so by taking a niacin supplement you'll short-circuit that production. By considering all three aspects, the program is effective while it calls for only moderate dietary modification, a small amount of oat bran, and reasonable doses of niacin.

This diary is specifically designed to help you implement the details of the program explained in *The 8-Week Cholesterol Cure*. For many people, reading and understanding what needs to be done and actually going out and doing it are two different things. Without an established discipline, people often find it hard to adhere to the program no matter how good their intentions are. In other cases, it simply seems like too many new things to be concerned about all at once. Try to think of this diary as a helping hand in taking that all-important first step towards a healthier lifestyle.

After all, for most people, when it comes to percentages and figures and numbers about nutrition, the eyes just glaze over. Who can understand or remember all those numbers? When you add in reminders about getting enough soluble fiber and taking niacin tablets regularly, plus advice about regular exercise and cutting down on stress, it sounds like a lot of details to follow.

For example, the American Heart Association says that everyone in the United States should limit their cholesterol intake to no more than 300 milligrams a day. And the fat intake should be no more than 30 percent of total calories, with 10 percent each coming from saturated fat, polyunsaturated fat, and monounsaturated fat. Confusing? You bet. What does all that mean in the real world of shopping for and eating food?

Most people find it tough just to remember how many calories different foods have; it's hard to memorize calorie charts. The majority of us just learn that some foods are more "fattening" than others.

Even then, there are many misconceptions. For example, many people believe that butter has more calories than margarine; actually they are identical. Or that pasta and baked potatoes are fattening. Actually, it's only the fats we may put on those foods that add up the calories.

But, even if we don't know *anything* about calories, we can see the results in the mirror and on the bathroom scale. It's not quite so simple with cholesterol. Too many people don't know their levels are dangerously high until the doctor says it's time for bypass surgery.

This diary is designed in part to help you become familiar with the numbers that you need to know, and to help you incorporate heart-healthy habits into part of your everyday routine. The first step towards change is gaining a better awareness of your current habits. You can't really improve your diet until you know exactly how good or bad it is to start with. You can't reduce the stress in your life without first being aware of how much it is effecting you. And you may not be able to stick to this program unless you establish clear goals for yourself and monitor your progress, day by day.

You will find once you begin the program that it is not as daunting as it sounds at first. But before we get into the actual details of how to use this diary to help you keep track of all those numbers, I want you to think about something obvious. We all learn things a little bit at a time. Today we can all tell the difference between an inch and a mile, and between an ounce and a gallon. We know that something weighs "about a pound," and that another thing is "about six inches long." We've learned those things by experience over the years. It'll take a little time, but you can also learn the numbers that can help you lower your cholesterol and keep it low. And this diary will help you along the way, so that you can be sure that you are doing all you can to follow the program properly without unnecessarily disrupting your lifestyle. The following pages provide an overview of *The 8-Week Cholesterol Cure.* If you've read the book, don't skip this material; read it as a refresher. If you haven't read the book, read this material as an overview, and then get all the details from the book itself.

Cholesterol Testing

The first step is knowing what your cholesterol level is. The National Cholesterol Education Program has recommended that everyone over twenty should have his or her level tested and that everyone should aim for a measurement of 200 mg/dl or less.

With new techniques testing has become quite widespread. In addition to the traditional hospital or laboratory, where samples of blood are drawn by needle through a vein in the arm, supermarkets, shopping malls, and health fairs host fingerprick testing sessions, during which you can learn your cholesterol level in minutes.

Unfortunately, such convenience brings with it a few problems. The fingerprick test may or may not be accurate and it doesn't give the important HDL/total cholesterol ratio. Some people are erroneously frightened into cholesterol-reducing programs, while others are wrongly reassured that their cholesterol levels are just fine, and so they continue with current lifestyles. And even the standard tests are not always accurate. Your best bet is to rely on the trend shown by two or three tests rather than just one.

A number of years ago, researchers found that the total cholesterol in the blood could be broken down into a number of fractions, determined by the lipoproteins, which carry cholesterol: low-density lipoprotein cholesterol (LDL), very-low-density lipoprotein cholesterol (VLDL), and high-density lipoprotein cholesterol (HDL).

Low-density lipoprotein cholesterol (LDL) is generally regarded as the real culprit in coronary heart disease. LDL carries cholesterol through the blood and deposits it in the arteries in a mass of calcium, fibers, and other substances collectively referred to as plaque. The formation of such plaque is called atheroma, and the disease is atherosclerosis. It is this atherosclerosis that we commonly call coronary heart disease. The higher the level of LDL, the greater the risk of heart disease occurring.

Very-low-density lipoprotein cholesterol (VLDL) is the substance used by the liver to manufacture LDL. Scientists refer to VLDL as a precursor of LDL. In other words, the higher the level of VLDL, the more LDL that can be produced by the liver.

High-density lipoprotein cholesterol (HDL) is the protective fraction of cholesterol. HDL actually acts to draw cholesterol away from the linings of arteries. The higher the HDL level, the more protection against heart disease. The ratio between total cholesterol and HDL cholesterol, or between LDL cholesterol and HDL cholesterol, is extremely important. The higher the ratio, the greater the risk of heart disease, since there is far more LDL trying to line the arteries than there is HDL trying to keep the cholesterol away from the arteries.

HDL cholesterol, in fact, may be a more important consideration in many cases than even total cholesterol or LDL cholesterol. Studying this issue at the University of California at Berkeley, researchers concluded that increased LDLs and decreased HDLs are both associated with a higher incidence of heart disease. But the importance of LDL levels was reduced when HDL was taken into consideration; that is to say, HDL was more predictive of heart disease than LDL.

The immediate implication of this information about HDL cholesterol levels is that you shouldn't rely entirely on tests that measure only total cholesterol. The best bet is to ask your doctor to refer you to a good laboratory where you can learn about your HDLs as well as your LDLs and triglycerides. Anyone who has been found to have a total cholesterol level much over 200 should definitely have a more revealing lipoprotein analysis performed. Then you can discuss the best approaches of control with your physician.

When you do have a fingerprick test done, rest for about five to ten minutes. Then make sure your hands are nice and warm. If the fingers are cold, blood won't flow very well and the technician may try to "milk" blood from the fingertip. This compromises accuracy by giving readings significantly lower owing to the dilution of the sample.

Virtually every authority agrees that one should trust a trend in cholesterol values rather than a single reading. Fingerprick testing can certainly provide that kind of trend, and is valuable in terms of screening the public and for monitoring one's progress. Authorities now strongly recommend that individuals who find themselves at supposed risk as the result of a cholesterol test ought to have the test repeated.

To have the lipoprotein analysis done accurately, patients should fast for twelve to fourteen hours prior to having their blood drawn in the laboratory. While the food eaten just prior to testing will have little if any influence on cholesterol levels as such, it can elevate triglycerides, which are the storage form of fats in the blood. Those triglycerides, in turn, are used in the laboratory to calculate the amount of LDL cholesterol.

The goal is to have a ratio of total cholesterol to HDL cholesterol below 4.5. As an example, a total cholesterol of 240 and an HDL level of 80 gives a ratio of 3.0. The ratio can be affected by either raising the HDL or lowering the LDL. The latter is more practical. The 4.5 ratio is the level associated with the standard risk of women, who have far less heart disease than men. Even better is a ratio of 3.5, which is associated with half the standard risk for men. No one should be satisfied until the total cholesterol is less than 200 or at least until the ratio is less than 4.5. And anyone undertaking cholesterol reduction should do so under medical supervision, in order to be safe and effective.

Beginning the Program

The recommendation from all authorities is that the place to begin a cholesterol-lowering program is with better diet. The goal is to stick to a diet that both reduces LDL levels and protects or raises the HDL levels. This means a diet low in fats and cholesterol and reduced in total calories.

The next thing to do is to quit smoking cigarettes. Every study done in this area shows that smokers have consistently lower HDL levels than non-smokers. While you're at it, stay away from smokers as much as possible. It appears that even passive smoking by way of other people's smoldering cigarettes can reduce HDL levels. Sadly, children of smokers have lower HDL counts than do those in homes with nonsmoking parents.

If you're overweight, try to bring your weight down to normal. Looking at the data from the Multiple Risk Factor Intervention Trial, researchers have reported that weight loss results in both a decrease in LDL and an increase in HDL—by as much as 5 milligrams, which can be enough to protect against heart disease.

Virtually every study has shown that moderate alcohol intake is associated with elevated HDL levels. Some have even postulated that this may be the reason we see moderate drinkers enjoying longer lives than teetotalers. Moderate drinking has been defined as one or two drinks daily, taken as wine, beer, or mixed drinks.

No one, including myself, believes that current nondrinkers should be encouraged to start imbibing in order to increase their HDL levels. The potential harm of alcohol consumption, including liver disease, alcoholism, and accidents, must be taken into consideration. But for those who currently enjoy a cocktail before dinner or a glass or two of wine or beer during the meal, there's no reason not to continue the pleasant ritual.

Sufficient quantities of oat bran or other forms of soluble fiber ingested on a regular basis have been shown to produce dramatic lowering of total cholesterol without harming HDL levels. And for those people who are unable to reduce their cholesterol through diet alone, niacin treatment can produce a significant lowering of LDL production and an increase in the amount and proportions of the protective HDL.

Furthermore, numerous studies have shown that a program of regular, moderate aerobic exercise can increase HDL levels. Exercise can also be helpful in alleviating stress, which has been shown to increase cholesterol levels.

Early research done with cholesterol-lowering diets showed that increasing the amount of polyunsaturated fats could significantly drop total cholesterol levels. Many advocated significant increases in consumption of cooking oils rich in polyunsaturated fatty acids, such as corn oil and safflower oil. Now we know that, while total cholesterol levels do drop with this approach, so do HDL numbers. Today there's agreement that monounsaturated fats are the better way to go. When used to replace saturated fats in the diet, monounsaturated fats such as olive oil can lower cholesterol while preserving HDLs.

We also now know that very-low-fat diets can significantly lower the levels of the protective HDLs. The benefit to total cholesterol reduction may be completely offset by concomitant drops in HDLs. That's often the case when following such regimens as the Pritikin Program. Very seldom does one achieve such dramatic reduction in total cholesterol, down to, say, 130 to 140 mg/dl, that the need for HDLs diminishes. Most followers of such programs see only moderate cholesterol reduction, accompanied by drops in HDL. That's why I recommend a more moderate approach, along with the increased consumption of foods that will selectively lower LDLs while sparing HDLs entirely.

A Sound Diet

The purpose of a good diet is to provide all the nutrients we need to live a hearty, robust life. Those nutrients help us maintain and, in the case of children, grow our bodies. After all, what is the purpose of eating? Basically, we should eat to live. Too many have learned to live to eat. It's time to get back to basics.

While the plan has been criticized from time to time for being too simplistic, the basic four-food-group approach remains an excellent guideline for selecting foods. Adults need a minimum of two servings from the meat and dairy groups and four servings each from the fruit/vegetable and grain groups. Is this plan possible and practical for a calorie-and-cholesterol conscious person? Definitely, if one remembers the advice to consume a *wide variety* of foods from these groups. And the plan comes to life when stressing the importance of the latter two groups of foods. Stress the word *minimum* in the four servings.

In order to get all the protein needed, two servings from the meat group are completely sufficient. Some find it more accurate to call this the protein group, since it also includes protein sources such as poultry, fish, and beans.

Is there anything wrong with beef? Or with any of the other red meats? Absolutely not, if eaten in moderation. But what constitutes a "serving" of meat? It's not a sixteen-ounce steak! A serving of meat should be no more than four ounces. And it's really not asking that much to trim the excess fat from the edges.

Next we come to the dairy group. Milk products are an excellent source of calcium, protein, and vitamins A and D. But those nutrients do not reside in the fat. Low-fat or nonfat varieties of milk, yogurt, and cheese have all the same nutrients. Often they cost less. And, if at first your taste buds don't respond favorably, give yourself a little time to get used to the lightness of the reduced-fat dairy foods. After a while, believe it or not, one actually comes to prefer the more healthful types.

When it comes to the fruit/vegetable group, there's no limit at all to what you may eat as long as you don't start gaining weight. Orange juice, for all its vitamin C, is also pretty heavy on calories. On the other hand, since you've cut down on fats, you can make up for those calories with fresh fruits of all types. Go into a good food store or a fresh-fruit-and-vegetable store and treat yourself to a shopping bag full of fresh treats.

Finally, the grain group. Now you can forget all the old rules about avoiding those so-called "fattening" starches. Eat rice and rolls and bread if you want to—every single day. Don't even worry about the calories. And remember, in Europe and other countries where bread is considered a staple of life and a source of national pride, no one puts butter on the bread. It takes away from the taste of the bread itself. When it comes to pasta, go wild. Enjoy all the forms and varieties you can find.

Since I started to cut down on fats, I don't have to count calories. Now I can eat all the food I want, with practically no limits. Instead I count the milligrams of cholesterol and the amount of fat in the foods I select. These are really the only numbers you need to concentrate on. But you have to remember to watch both your cholesterol *and* your fat consumption. A lot of foods are now emblazoned with labels that say "no cholesterol" in big letters, even though they may still contain much more fat than you need. You have to keep careful count of both these numbers. The aim is to keep your fat and cholesterol intake low, the lower the better. No matter what else one may do to reduce cholesterol levels in the blood, the place to start is with the diet.

To help you start counting those grams and milligrams, you'll find some charts of commonly eaten foods and the amounts of fats and cholesterol found in typical serving sizes at the back of this diary. You will also see that every day features a Food Journal section. By writing down everything you eat and then referring to the charts at the back of the book, you can keep track of your exact fat and cholesterol consumption on a daily basis. Not only will this help you tell very specifically whether you are staying within your limits, but just going through the process of looking up the numbers on what you ate will help you familiarize yourself with the numbers you need to know very quickly. The hope is that after using this diary for eight weeks, you will know which foods to concentrate on and which to avoid, and won't need to go through exact calculations anymore. You'll find that you will naturally gravitate towards those foods with low levels of fats and cholesterol without checking the guideline charts at all.

To use the food journal effectively, first you have to set targets for yourself so you know exactly how many milligrams of cholesterol and grams of fat and how many calories you want to allow yourself every day. Once you understand how the process works, you'll see that it's not complicated at all. Let's start with something very basic: how to figure out how much food to eat to stay healthy and at ideal body weight. Only two variables come into play: first, whether you're a man or woman; second, whether you're sedentary, moderately active, or very active. Then decide your ideal weight. The weight table at the back of the diary was adapted from the Metropolitan Life Insurance Company of New York, and specifies weights most health authorities have accepted as beneficial for optimum health.

The next step is to decide to feed *only* your ideal weight, *not* the weight you have today—unless, of course, you are already at ideal weight. If you weigh, let's say, 175 pounds and should weigh 150 pounds, then feed only your 150-pound self; let the other 25 pounds slowly drift away.

An adult man with a moderately active lifestyle will require 15 calories for every pound of his weight. If he starts to become involved with a real strenuous exercise program, he may need an extra calorie per pound. If he becomes sedentary, like so many men in the United States, he'll burn even fewer than 15 calories per pound.

Women unfortunately have different metabolisms, and, for the most part, they burn fewer calories per pound. A moderately active woman needs only 12 calories per pound of ideal body weight.

The calculations, then, are rather simple:

Moderately active man
150 pounds x 15 calories/pound = 2250 calories/day

Relatively unactive man
150 pounds x 13 calories/pound = 1950 calories/day

Moderately active woman
120 pounds x 12 calories/pound = 1440 calories/day

Relatively unactive woman
120 pounds x 10 calories/pound = 1200 calories/day

For a specific example, let's look at a moderately active male of middle age. Our sample specimen weighs 150 pounds to match his 5-foot-10-inch frame. Or he wants to weigh 150 pounds in which case he should feed only the pounds he wants. So he'll need 15 calories to maintain each of those 150 pounds. Let's do the mathematics:

$$150 \text{ pounds} \times 15 \text{ calories} = 2250 \text{ calories per day}$$

Now we need to know how much fat he can consume every day. In my program I recommend a middle-ground level of 20 percent fat intake. If your cholesterol is not too high you may find that you can increase the percentage to say, 25 percent of calories as fat (but you should not exceed 30 percent in any case). Those at real risk should considering cutting down to just 10 percent. Let's take the middle ground and say that of those 2250 calories we want our man to have 20 percent as fat. That bit of math is just as simple:

$$2250 \text{ calories} \times .20 = 450 \text{ calories as fat}$$

But how do we get from calories to grams of fat? One gram of protein or carbohydrate yields 4 calories. One gram of fat yields 9 calories (and some believe as much as 10 or 12 calories). Therefore, 450 calories will come from 50 grams of fat, as determined in this simple calculation:

$$450 \text{ calories} \div 9 \text{ calories per gram} = 50 \text{ grams}$$

Now it's time to plug your own numbers into the equations to determine your target fat intake as measured in grams. Multiply by 10 calories if you are a sedentary adult woman; by 11 calories if you are a sedentary adult man; by 12 calories if you're a moderately active woman; or by 15 calories if you are a moderately active man. By multiplying your ideal weight by the appropriate number of calories per pound, you'll have the number of calories you need to maintain your ideal weight.

$$\underline{\hspace{0.5cm} 110 \hspace{0.5cm}} \qquad \underline{\hspace{0.5cm} 12 \hspace{0.5cm}} \qquad \underline{\hspace{0.5cm} 1220 \hspace{0.5cm}}$$
ideal weight   x   calories per pound   =   daily calories

$$\underline{\hspace{0.5cm} 1220 \hspace{0.5cm}} \text{ x } .20 = \underline{\hspace{0.5cm} 244 \hspace{0.5cm}}$$
daily calories   daily calories as fat

$$\underline{\hspace{0.5cm} 244 \hspace{0.5cm}} \div 9 = \underline{\hspace{0.5cm} 27 \hspace{0.5cm}}$$
daily calories as fat   daily grams of fat

Obviously, if you are very sedentary on the one hand, or if you get turned on by heavy-duty exercise on the other, your caloric needs will be different. But, for the most part, these are the caloric needs for the male and female examples I've chosen.

Now we know our male example will be allowed a target total of 50 grams of fat daily. He can count those grams easily by just looking at food nutrition labels, and by learning a bit about the amount of fat contained in some commonly consumed foods as shown in the table at the back of the book. Most foods today have very complete nutrition labels. Many magazines today provide complete nutrition breakdowns along with their recipes, listing the amount of fat, cholesterol, sodium, and calories provided per serving. *Family Circle* and *Woman's Day* are two good examples. You'll quickly see that foods with the most calories also have the most fat.

Carbohydrates and proteins contain just 4 calories per gram. There are about 28 grams to an ounce, for those who don't "think metric." But fat contains 9 calories per gram! If you just cut down on the amount of fat you eat, you'll automatically and dramatically reduce calories.

The table at the end of this book clearly states the amount of fat, cholesterol, sodium, and calories found in commonly used foods. Some shellfish have considerable amounts of cholesterol, though still much lower than previously believed. These foods, however, have very low levels of fat. So they can be enjoyed in moderation as long as they are not fried.

You don't have to try to memorize these charts, but do become familiar with trends in composition for types of foods. Certainly it is not possible to list all the thousands of foods found in the supermarket. If you'd like to have a more complete listing, I'd recommend the book *Food Values of Portions Commonly Used* by Jean A. T. Pennington and Helen Nichols Church. The book, published by Harper & Row, is considered a bible by anyone involved in food and nutrition. You'll be amazed, as time goes by, how easy it will be to choose one food over another because of the numbers you'll learn.

Do some other comparisons in the chart. Note that while turkey breast and beef cuts contain just about the same amount of cholesterol in a 3 1/2-ounce serving, the difference in the amount of fat is enormous. One serving of turkey provides less than 2 grams, while the same weight of porterhouse steak gives you nearly 15 grams!

But does that mean you can't ever have a piece of beef? Certainly not. Just remember that you want to keep your total fat consumption and cholesterol intake down on a daily basis. If you want a piece of steak for the evening meal, cut down on fat in the rest of your foods that day. And choose the cuts of beef lower in fat content.

Since few foods, however, list cholesterol content, you will need to take some time to learn where that cholesterol lurks. Your target is to stay under 250 milligrams daily. With some foods, that's a real problem while for others it's not at all. An egg yolk contains about 250 milligrams of cholesterol all by itself.

You'll be surprised how quickly you'll learn the cholesterol levels of foods so that you won't have to consult the chart every time you bite into something. At the beginning, though, you'll also be surprised to see cholesterol in foods you never even thought of as culprits.

As long as you stay within your target figures, you can eat any combination of foods you choose. Using the food journal to record what you're eating will help you quickly become aware of where the cholesterol is in *your* diet, and will help you focus on the foods you need to cut down on.

How much cholesterol could there be in cornbread made from a mix? After all, there's no cholesterol in corn. But thanks to other things added, such as lard and dried egg yolks, cornbread and other bakery mixes are significant sources of fat and cholesterol. Pancakes have about 33 milligrams of cholesterol *each*; and how many do you have in a stack? But all is not lost. Just start making your pancakes with egg whites instead. No problem; they're delicious. And French toast made with egg substitute can't be distinguished from those slices made with whole eggs. A little bit of awareness and imagination can go a long way towards a big improvement in your diet, without deprivation.

Food Journal

Although this diet plan is relatively simple and with time becomes easy to follow, many people have trouble with compliance in the early stages. Some find it difficult to keep track of the new numbers; others simply find it hard to modify their eating habits and comply with the principles of the program.

Often the hardest part is simply becoming aware of your regular eating habits. Most people are not used to paying strict attention to everything they eat. They may snack much more than they are aware of, or gulp down a second portion without even being conscious of it.

That's why when testing my 8-week program on patients and physicians under the auspices of the Santa Monica Hospital Medical Center, one of the first things we did was instruct everyone on how to keep a detailed food journal. We asked all the participants to keep a dietary diary for two weeks during the program. They listed all the foods and beverages consumed during each day. This served two purposes. First, we had a better idea of what people were actually eating. Second, the exercise was very educational. Often we don't realize what we're eating unless we actually list all those foods, step back, and take a look. After doing so, many were able to see where they were consuming fats and cholesterol they could easily reduce or replace.

The only way to control cholesterol permanently (and to lose weight permanently) is to change completely one's attitudes and approaches toward food. Certainly that's not easy, just as it isn't easy to quit smoking cigarettes. But both are necessary for anyone who really wants good health and long life.

More than anything else it is a simple matter of discipline. You have to understand your present habits, and reform the ones that are dangerous to you. The first step is to take a really close look at your current eating habits. As we did with the patients at the hospital, use the food journal portion of this book scrupulously for two straight weeks. You must record absolutely everything that you eat. Jot down even the tiniest nibble, and do it right when you are eating—don't wait until later and trust your memory.

Then look at your diary with objective eyes. What foods can be completely eliminated? What foods can you cut down on? What foods are you eating regularly that have large quantities of cholesterol and fat? Check your fat and cholesterol consumption against the target levels that you computed for yourself. Review the recommendations from earlier in this book, and from *The 8-Week Cholesterol Cure*. At the same time, check to see if you are keeping within the calorie limit that you figured out for yourself.

For the next week or two, concentrate on making adjustments in your eating patterns. Continue to keep the journal just as carefully. See how much you've improved. Ask yourself whether there are foods that really don't belong on your table anymore. Many overweight individuals have no idea how many calories they take in each day while snacking. Keep that diet diary and you will see for yourself. Is the midnight snack your downfall? Do you destroy all your good intentions with a candy bar in the evening? Is there one particular food or time of day that is a problem for you? By the end of the eight-week period in this diary, you should be able to monitor and reform your eating habits to conform to our recommendations.

For many people, the simple discipline of keeping the diary regularly is enough to help them modify their diet without drastically changing their lives. After all, discipline is a key to changing any pattern in your life. When a cholesterol-healthy diet becomes a natural habit rather than a chore, you've come a long way.

Food Groups

When reviewing your diet journal, you should also take a careful look at how the foods you are eating break down into those four basic food groups that we talked about earlier. Remember that you need two servings from each group, with unlimited servings from the fruit and vegetable group and the grains group. Make sure that you are satisfying your body's basic needs, and look to see if you are consistently exceeding your limits in any one area—having too many portions of meat on a regular basis, for example.

Using the food groups as a reference point will help to remind you of the substitutions that you can make. For example, maybe one of those meat dishes can be replaced by a nice bowl of pasta. If you see that you are eating too much meat and not enough vegetables and grains, by adding a big salad and some bread to your dinner you may be happy with a much smaller portion of meat. There is a wealth of delicious foods you can draw on that will keep you both healthy and feeling full. By using the food groups as a reference point, you'll help remind yourself of the many options for good nutrition.

Fluids

The best part of having oat-bran muffins as a staple of your diet is that they are incredibly satisfying. The reason is that oat bran absorbs a lot of water in the digestive tract. As it soaks up the water, it expands, filling the stomach and giving one that satisfied full feeling.

Because of this property of oat bran, it's best to drink a lot of water when consuming a lot of oat bran. Eight eight-ounce glasses a day is best for everyone, regardless of other dietary considerations. The advice from your school nurse back in elementary school still holds today: You just can't drink too many fluids. If you don't like water, club soda with a squeeze of lime also counts, as do coffee, tea, and all other beverages. Make your selections wisely. Choose low-sodium club soda and decaffeinated coffee and tea. Limit the number of high-calorie beverages. A six-ounce serving of apple juice contains more than 90 calories. And, while beer and other alcoholic beverages do contain water, they also provide a lot of calories.

On the food journal page, you will see little icons representing the eight glasses of fluids you need every day. As you are recording what you have eaten, check off one box for each portion of fluids. While it is not essential that you meet the eight glass requirement all the time, this will help you get into the habit of keeping those fluids flowing.

Oat Bran

Of course, lowering total cholesterol and LDL cholesterol levels sufficiently by diet alone is probably not possible for most people with elevated levels. *The 8-Week Cholesterol Cure,* however, considers all three causes of elevated cholesterol. While it is still very important to modify the diet, eating oat bran and supplementing the diet with niacin will complete the cholesterol-lowering effect we all want.

Without describing in detail the research studies that back up the claims for oat bran, here's an overview of just what can be expected by making oat bran a part of the daily diet. Oat bran significantly lowers both total cholesterol and LDL cholesterol while not at all lowering the protective HDL levels. Investigations regarding oat bran have been conducted all over the world. Both animal and human studies have consistently demonstrated the significant effect oat bran has on cholesterol levels in the blood. Furthermore, the longer one stays on a diet including oat bran, the greater the effects. In fact, even without restricting the diet radically, one can expect considerable lowering of cholesterol by simply eating three oat-bran muffins a day.

Can the same results be achieved with oatmeal? Since oat bran is one fraction of the oat flake, it would take more oatmeal than oat bran to achieve the same levels of lowering. There's no question, however, that oatmeal also exerts a cholesterol-lowering effect.

While oat bran used to be difficult to come by, it is now available in just about every supermarket and health-food store nationally. For the most part it comes packaged in one-pound boxes, and can be found in the hot-cereal sections of the store. While Quaker was the first to put oat bran on the market, a number of other companies have followed suit in the past few years. The package should list just one ingredient: oat bran.

The amount that I advocate consuming daily is one-half cup, uncooked, as it comes out of the box. That's less than 2 ounces, or about 50 grams. But by all means feel free to eat more. You can't eat too much oat bran when it's baked in muffins, breads, rolls, cakes, cookies, and other foods naturally suited to it. Try the recipes in *The 8-Week Cholesterol Cure Cookbook.* Then think of your own favorites. Whenever a recipe calls for breadcrumbs or coatings, try oat bran instead.

If you happen to be a baker, or are lucky enough to live with one or have one as a good friend, oat bran offers a whole world of delicious possibilities. When I first began restricting my diet to things that were "good for me," I did rather miss the goodies. But as time has gone on, I've found so many alternatives that I don't feel a bit deprived. I eat cakes, brownies, cookies, and all sorts of other treats. I don't even have to worry about the calories. For once, the things you *should* eat taste as good as the things you *want* to eat.

Before you put any food into your shopping cart, first read the label. Often you'll see that oat bran is one of the last ingredients listed, meaning that there just isn't much of it in these products. That goes for some of the top name-brand cereals. If oat bran isn't the number one ingredient listed on the label, don't rely on that food as a major source of your soluble fiber. Oat flour contains little or no soluble fiber: remember that the flour is the fraction left over after milling for oat bran. And "oat fiber" often means not oat bran but rather the non-digestible fiber from the hull of the grain, containing no soluble fiber. Is it best to eat all the oat bran at once, say at breakfast, or would you be better off with some cereal and other soluble fiber-rich foods throughout the day? The soluble fiber of oat bran works in the digestive tract by binding the bile acids, which are made from cholesterol. Those bile acids are made throughout the day. Thus by eating oat-bran muffins and other foods throughout the day, one has a better chance of cholesterol reduction.

The same ingredient that makes oat bran so effective, the soluble fiber, can also be found in a number of other foods, including rice bran, apple bran, dried beans and peas, prunes, and even guar gum.

That's why the box on the diary pages titled "Oat Bran" is also called "Soluble Fiber." Personally, I prefer to eat my three oat bran muffins a day and know that I am consuming my 50 grams of oat bran. For those who do likewise, there are three little boxes that you can check off, one for each muffin. Many people, however, will choose to meet their soluble fiber requirements in other ways. Many of the recipes in *The 8-Week Cholesterol Cure Cookbook* show you a number of delicious ways of working soluble fiber into your diet. For those people, the blank lines can by used to record the amount of whatever kind of soluble fiber you do consume, to ensure that you remember to meet your requirements in one form or another every day.

Niacin

When the government-sponsored panel of health specialists met in Washington, D.C., in October 1987 to "declare war on cholesterol," they pointed out that not everyone would be able to get his or her cholesterol level under the desired 200-mg limit by diet alone. Some may need to have drugs

19

prescribed, and they also pointed out that for many people niacin should be considered as a first line of treatment.

The medical literature is filled with success stories in which cholesterol levels fall anywhere between 10 and 25 percent for those taking niacin alone or in combination with other approaches. Just taking niacin alone, without any changes in diet or lifestyle, is enough to produce a significant lowering of total cholesterol levels. And when taken along with a sensible, modified-fat diet niacin produces even more dramatic results. Niacin acts to lower LDL and VLDL production in the liver and to increase the amount and proportions of the protective HDL in the blood.

The program advocated in this book is the same recommended by some of the nation's most prestigious scientific and medical organizations. For some, diet, especially diet including oat bran and other water-soluble fibers, may be enough to get cholesterol levels down sufficiently. But, for many others niacin is the treatment of choice.

Niacin has long been available in practically every health-food store, drugstore, and pharmacy, and it comes in a variety of strengths and formulations. While suggested dosages vary, I have found that 3 grams of niacin in its regular formulation, or 1.5 grams in the new time-release formulation, is the maximum amount needed.

These dosage schedules have been widely published in the medical literature and provide physicians with a general approach. However, owing to individual variations and needs, your physician may wish to modify dosage in your case. Do not begin niacin treatment without his or her medical supervision.

I am so enthusiastic about this time-release formulation that I now strongly recommend it over the other kinds of niacin. If you do prefer to take niacin in its regular formulation, please refer to *The 8-Week Cholesterol Cure* for detailed information about how to find the proper dosage for yourself, and the side-effects such as flushing that you may experience.

The product I use, known as Endur-acin, is a sustained-release niacin. The niacin very slowly trickles out of a wax matrix tablet, more smoothly than has ever been achieved before. Because of this smooth-release pattern, two wonderful things occur. First, for the vast majority of people, the flushing sensation often associated with taking niacin is eliminated. Second, the dosage needed to achieve dramatic effects is drastically reduced. The very few individuals who may experience a slight flush with Endur-acin are in the distinct minority.

Begin with one 500-milligram tablet taken at the evening meal. Assuming that you experience no difficulties or discomfort, after one week add another tablet with lunch. Then after a week taking the 1000-milligram total, go on to the three tablets, one 500-milligram tablet three times daily. Your physician may decide to alter this to fit your needs.

Endur-acin can be ordered directly from the manufacturer, the Endurance Products Company in Oregon. They have made the product available to the public through a separate company for mail-order sales. I'm particularly pleased that the cost for this very high-quality product is extremely reasonable, often cheaper than ordinary niacin found in health-food stores. If you're interested in obtaining a supply of Endur-acin, you may write for ordering information to:

Endurance Products Co.
P.O. Box 230489
Portland, OR 97223

Certain people should not take niacin at all. Contraindications for taking this vitamin in large doses include active peptic ulcer, liver disease, severe heart arrhythmias, diabetes, and gout. Interestingly, however, physicians have told me they have given Endur-acin to patients with diabetes and even mild cases of gout without difficulty. Certainly though, such patients should be closely monitored by their physicians. In fact, *anyone deciding to use niacin as part of their cholesterol-lowering program should be sure to inform his or her physician first. Niacin should be taken only under medical supervision.*

If you do start taking niacin, after a period of time—say, two months or so—you should have a blood test to check the function of the liver. Actually, this is not at all inconvenient since you will want to check your cholesterol level to determine progress by that time anyway. The tests will show how well the liver is metabolizing the niacin. For the vast majority of people, there will be no problem at all. Repeat the cholesterol and liver function tests at six months, at one year, and annually thereafter.

Niacin can be an important part of your program to reduce serum cholesterol. Along with a modified diet including oat bran, niacin has been shown to be safe and effective. I've been particularly edified that in the past years since *The 8-Week Cholesterol Cure* was originally published an increasing number of physicians have begun to write the words "8-Week Cholesterol Cure" on their prescription pads and to instruct their patients to follow the program and to come back in eight weeks. While my program continues to have its critics, the number of doctors who have seen the program's safety and efficacy continues to grow.

The niacin box in this journal is there to serve as a simple reminder for those who are taking niacin. For people just starting the program it's often difficult to remember if they have taken their tablets for the day. Just check off the little pill symbol every time you take your niacin. If you are taking niacin around mealtime, it should be easy to check it off as you are recording what you have eaten. Like counting your cholesterol and fat intake, remembering to take your pills will soon become second nature.

If you decide to include niacin in your program to lower serum cholesterol levels, be sure to inform your physician.

Exercise

Those sweating masses appear to be on the right track. Dr. Ralph Paffenbarger, speaking of his research published in the March 6, 1986 *New England Journal of Medicine*, said those who regularly exercise throughout their lives add from one to more than two years to their lives. Those are average numbers, with some individuals expected to tack on ten or even twenty years of living. Put another way, Dr. Paffenbarger said that every hour spent exercising will be returned in added life, with an extra hour as a dividend. You just can't beat that kind of investment.

Three separate studies have now provided definitive proof that regular aerobic exercise improves the health of the heart. These research studies used animals rather than people for the very simple reason that animals could be sacrificed so their hearts could be examined. Exercise also has a beneficial effect on HDL levels.

Looking at the improvement in lipid profiles of those involved with a cardiac rehabilitation program, researchers in West Virginia found that exercising three times weekly for three months resulted in an increase of up to 7.5 percent in HDLs, with a rise from an average of 41.6 mg/dl to 44.3 mg/dl. The patients exercised at 70 to 80 percent of their maximum heart rate. Some research indicates even moderate exercise has good effects on HDLs. A study reported in the *Journal of the American Medical Association* indicates that's even true for older men and women.

Researchers at the National Defense University in Washington, D.C., examined the relationship between miles run per week and HDL levels in 1020 healthy males with an average age of 43 years. They found that optimal changes in lipid levels occur when a person runs an average of sixteen miles a week; that is, LDL levels go down a bit, and HDL levels rise. That comes out to be about three miles a day, five days a week, which is not terribly much if you're a runner. Running more than that didn't further improve HDL levels. On the other hand, running less than nine miles weekly produced no beneficial effects in terms of HDLs.

No matter what you weigh or how many calories you are consuming, it's important to keep the metabolic rate up. A frustrating phenomenon that occurs when people try to diet is that the body compensates for reduced food intake by burning calories more slowly. Actually this is the body's natural way to deal with times of famine and starvation. When there is less food available, less energy is consumed and burned by the tissues.

To get around this, one must become more active, to reach the next level of calorie burning. For most people this can be done merely by taking a walk once a day. Writing in the *Journal of the American Medical Association*, in May 1988, Dr. James Rippe recommended walking for health and fitness. He noted that even low-to-moderate levels of exercise, when done regularly, provide important cardiovascular health benefits. Brisk walking provides strenuous enough exercise, he says, for cardiovascular training in most adults. Walking has been shown to reduce anxiety and tension and to aid in weight loss. And done regularly, walking can improve cholesterol ratios by elevating HDL levels.

The importance of inactivity is becoming more apparent because so many men and women do not do enough aerobic exercise. Yes, smoking is probably a more significant risk factor—but only 18 percent of our population currently smokes cigarettes. Yes, hypertension is probably a more significant risk factor—but only 10 percent of the adults have asystolic blood pressure level above 150. The bottom line is that 80 to 90 percent of our population still do not do sufficient cardiovascular exercise.

A beneficial side effect of exercise is that those who get actively engaged in such activities as swimming and jogging tend to quit smoking cigarettes. This is true even for those who have smoked for years and who have tried to quit before.

Then, of course, there's weight loss. Exercise should be an integral part of any weight-loss program. It appears that exercise speeds up the metabolism in such a way that calories are burned more efficiently for hours afterward. The result is pounds lost even when one is eating the same amount of food.

A final benefit also involves cholesterol, but in an indirect way. Stress raises cholesterol levels and has been considered a significant risk factor in heart disease. Exercise, it turns out, can effectively reduce stress, and, in turn, cholesterol.

One measure of heart-healthy physical fitness is the rate at which your heart beats at rest, that is, when you are not exercising. The average heart rate is about 72 beats per minute. Well-trained athletes get their rates well below 60, and often under 50.

The easiest way to check your own rate is to hold a finger to the carotid artery in your neck. You can feel it pulsing next to the windpipe. Count the beats per minute with a sweep-second watch or clock. Then you can use that figure to see how you progress. As you become more fit, your resting rate will fall.

Once you've gotten your doctor's approval to begin a program of cardiovascular fitness, you'll want to do some exercise that will increase your heart rate. But how much is enough and how much is too much?

First you can determine the maximum heart rate for your age simply by subtracting your age from the number 220. That will give you, in practical terms, the absolute capacity of your heart to beat. Of course you don't want to exercise at that maximum rate since that would severely strain your heart, perhaps even to the point of death. Instead, multiply that number by 65 percent; this is the level at which you want to exercise in the beginning, occasionally checking your heart rate as you do your workout.

$$220 - \underset{\text{your age}}{\underline{65}} = \underset{\text{your maximum heart rate}}{\underline{155}}$$

$$\text{(maximum heart rate)} \times .65 = \underset{\substack{\text{target heart rate when} \\ \text{you start exercising}}}{\underline{100.75}}$$

Gradually work your ability up to 70 percent, then to 75 percent, and finally on to 80 percent. You don't want to exceed 80 percent of your maximum heart-rate potential; that's your training rate.

To reap the benefit of exercise, do it a minimum of three days weekly at your desired training rate for at least thirty minutes. First do a bit of warmup, perhaps some stretching exercises, and then on to thirty minutes at your training rate. It's best to do such exercise four or five times per week. In fact, the rule of thumb is that you need four to five days to gain, and three days per week to maintain, fitness.

What kind of exercise is best? Basically any kind of strenuous workout—jogging, energetic walking, swimming, various sports—you enjoy is fine. The important thing is to make a commitment to exercise regularly, three to five days each and every week.

If you haven't done any physical exercise in quite a while, be certain to start off slowly and gradually increase your tolerance. Especially if there has been any family history of heart disease or if you are over the age of thirty-five it's best to check with your physician before starting off on an exercise program.

It's a funny thing, but people seem to have a very short memory when it comes to remembering when they last exercised. Wasn't it yesterday, or maybe two days ago at the longest? Often the memory plays tricks on us, and invariably we allow more time to pass between exercise sessions than we should—unless we write it down. In this diary, it's there for you to see, every day. When you see the exercise journal, you'll be reminded of the work you need to do, and with the flip of one or two pages you'll easily know if you've been derelict or not.

But there's a pleasurable side to this organizational device as well. As you begin a regular exercise program, you will quickly see signs of tangible improvement. Soon, you'll be exercising at a higher percentage of your maximum heart rate. You'll be able to exercise longer, without getting tired. And your resting pulse will decline.

Every time you exercise, take your resting pulse first. Make sure you do some stretches and warm-up exercises first—you should never just start right in with heavy exercising. After five to ten minutes you should have your pulse up to the target rate that you've set for yourself, and you want to keep exercising for twenty to thirty minutes at that target rate. If your pulse goes too far above the target rate, you are pushing yourself too far and need to slow down the activity. If your pulse is staying too low, then you need to increase your activity until you hit that target rate. If you ever start to feel dizzy or short of breath while exercising, stop whatever you are doing and give yourself a rest.

For that matter, anyone going on an exercise program who has been inactive for a while should consult with their physician first. It may take you longer than expected to build up to a healthy level of activity. But whatever kind of exercise you do and no matter what the pace, by keeping a careful record you can stick to your program and see just how far you have come.

Stress

Stress can be defined as any unpleasant emotion, be it anxiety, worry, anger, hostility, or pressures of many kinds. There's no way to eliminate all stress from our lives. Besides, we really wouldn't want to do so. A bit of stress has been shown to enhance performance, whether on an athletic field or during a college exam. Waiting for the winning number in a lottery has its own excitement. But there's a point where constructive stress gives way to a far more destructive form.

The case has often been cited of the accountants whose cholesterol levels were tested just before the April 15 tax deadline and two weeks afterward. There was a significant drop after the deadline. The same thing happened when medical school students were tested before and after examinations.

There we have the stress-cholesterol link. As much as we try to control the amount of cholesterol in our blood through the dietary aspects of this program, stress may be thwarting our good intentions. Stress takes its toll by contributing to a number of physical ailments including ulcers, headaches, stomach aches, colitis, and high blood pressure. It can make asthma and arthritis worse. Even sexual dysfunction can be traced to stress. And, it seems certain to say today, stress kills. In fact, Dr. Meyer Friedman first postulated that the Type A—or high-strung, anxious—individual is more prone to heart disease and elevated cholesterol levels than is the more relaxed Type B person. Friedman and his partner, Dr. Ray Rosenman, in the book *Type A Behavior and Your Heart,* recommend finding ways of changing behavior—of avoiding anger and time-driven stress factors—in order to reduce cholesterol levels. Clearly, the answer is to do something about reducing the effects of that stress.

Originally, Drs. Friedman and Rosenman gave the term Type A to those exhibiting a wide range of characteristics. Yet those characteristics didn't fit all the individuals having heart attacks. So investigators began to look at those characteristics individually rather than as a group. Today the evidence points primarily to two of those traits, namely anger and hostility.

Interestingly, many of the other characteristics of the Type A individual can often be explained by the traits of anger and hostility themselves. For example, if one becomes very time conscious, upset when someone is late or when waiting on a long line, that time consciousness really is a type of anger. The same can be applied to ambition. Certainly every successful person has a degree of ambition, but not all of them die of heart disease. The difference is whether one becomes hostile to those on the same career path.

There are three goals to shoot for in dealing with stress: (1) to reduce the number of stressful incidents, (2) to reduce the intensity of those episodes, and (3) to find ways to rest and relax in between. While it may be difficult, taking those three steps is not impossible.

Thus, one can be career-oriented, conscious of time constraints, and ambitious without necessarily doing damage, as long as one is not angry or hostile. Can it be done? I think all the work now on record showing that the Type A person can think in a more Type B mode indicates that the elements of anger and hostility can be tempered. All of the techniques of relaxation and stress reduction apply to toning down that anger and hostility.

The first thing to do is to become aware of your own stressors, the things that lead to your personal feelings of pressure and stress. Just as it is a good idea to keep a record of what you eat and drink when trying to modify the diet, it is very helpful to keep a log of daily stresses. That's why this book includes a section every day called the Stress Register.

As with the other record-keeping features in this diary, it is important that you make yourself more aware of when you are in a stressful situation and then record it. You need to learn to really focus on your own feelings and realize when you are feeling the anger and hostility that we talked about. Try to record it as it happens—without, of course, interfering with your regular activity. Then, as you review the other parts of this diary, take a close look for any patterns within your stress register.

Let's say that you record stress while driving to an appointment for which you might be late. Perhaps a way to deal with that is to leave ten or fifteen minutes earlier the next time. Maybe you can make the drive more pleasant by bringing along a cool drink and turning to a soothing music station on the car radio.

Your daily log may also show that you're going from one stressful episode right into another without having a chance to rest and recuperate in between. The body is a truly resilient machine, but such abuse can't go on for long without ill effect. If you think honestly about it, there must be a way to give yourself a "breather" when one stress ends and before another begins. Jot down your proposed strategy, and then implement that plan.

The next step is more difficult for the vast majority of fast-paced Americans. Learn to relax during those breathing spaces between stresses. For most people, that time is spent stewing about what made them anxious or angry in the first place, making matters worse as the mind allows the episode to gain even greater proportions.

There is no best prescription for relaxation. For some lucky men and women, it's enough to simply remind themselves to stop and smell the roses. For others, the old prescription of counting to ten really helps. But for most of us special efforts are needed.

Fortunately, professionals have come up with a number of techniques to help defuse the stress bomb. Practically every YMCA offers courses in yoga, meditation, and other relaxation methods. Such courses are also given at community hospitals and clinics, often at very low cost. A number of self-help books and tapes are available. And, for those who need special assistance along these lines, professionals can help with such techniques as biofeedback training or therapy and support groups.

Just as with the type of exercise you do, the trick is to find a relaxation technique that's right for you. It has to be something that fits your own lifestyle, and that you find actually enjoyable. Don't let your efforts to relax become yet another source of stress.

Diet and alcohol play important roles in terms of stress, since many people use both food and drink in dealing with their emotions. That heavy meal or enormous midnight snack eaten as consolation for a miserable day will only lead to a sleepless night. Ironically, the same thing applies to alcohol. While liquor in moderation can be enjoyable, it's not meant to be used as an anesthetic. Instead of leading to a good night's sleep, excessive alcohol intake results in poor rest and a terrible feeling in the morning.

Drinking coffee with caffeine is like pouring gasoline on a fire. The last thing one needs is jittery "coffee nerves." Try some of the new brewed decaffeinated coffees. The water-process types are particularly good since they avoid the use of chemicals.

Compare your notes about your stressful episodes from your stress register with those of a personality Type A. You're a Type A person if you overly stress certain words during conversations—driving the points home in case your listener doesn't catch them to your satisfaction. You do everything rapidly, both working and playing—never taking the time to savor the moment. You're impatient with how slowly everything takes place and you want to speed things along. You find it difficult to enjoy a conversation that doesn't have anything to do with your own interests or current lifestyle. You feel somewhat guilty about relaxing, thinking of work that could be done instead. You judge your own efforts in terms of numbers and you gauge progress by the clock and calendar, and somehow there's never enough time. You're more interested in things to have than enjoyable things to do. You find yourself doing or redoing the work of others because your standards so far exceed theirs. And you're certain that everything you've achieved is the result of your hard-driving personality. In short, you're the kind of person the world needs more of to be a better place!

If you're nodding your head "yes" to even a few of those traits, it's time to start thinking about how to reverse the process. Face the hard, cruel facts of life: if you died today, the world would go on without you. No man or woman is indispensable. *Yes*, you have time to go on vacation. *Yes*, that appointment can be postponed until later. *Yes*, your children will love you if you don't bring home as much bacon. *Yes*, it doesn't really matter if the appointment starts ten minutes late. You're not a horse with blinders leading your vision. You're a thinking human being who is smart enough to realize that, if you don't come to grips with the stresses around you, those stresses will come to grip you—around the heart.

An Overview

So let's review how you are going to use this diary to help you begin your cholesterol cure. First of all, you should complete the self-evaluation that precedes the diary pages. This gives you a chance to take stock of all the important factors and figures before you even start the program. There is another chart just like it at the end of the diary, so when you have made it through those first eight weeks you can see precisely how far you have come in that short period of time. It also gives you a chance to set revised goals for yourself as you continue your program.

It is essential that you get yourself in the habit of using the diary every day. Only by knowing exactly what you are eating can you be sure of bringing your diet into line. Once you get into the habit of following a low-fat, low-cholesterol diet, you will find yourself keeping track without even needing the diary.

Getting enough oat bran or other soluble fiber every day is very important. It can only work for you if you work at meeting your target consumption. Whether it's your three oat-bran muffins or one of the many other options available to you, keep track of this important part of your diet until it too becomes second nature.

If you choose to use niacin as part of your program and your doctor agrees, you must take your tablets regularly. There is no excuse for forgetting to take one of those tablets—once again, we've made it easier for you for those first eight weeks.

Don't take the exercise and stress sections lightly. These are areas that all of us could pay more attention to, regardless of our cholesterol levels. Simply put, most Americans do not get enough exercise to maintain healthy conditioning. Exercising in occasional bursts is not good enough. We could all use the dividends of longer, healthier life that exercise pays. As with changing your diet, discipline is an important part of a good exercise program. You don't have to climb that mountain all at once—make your way up one steady step at a time. Don't let yourself slide on exercise because you are doing so well in the other areas. Not only will you see your cholesterol levels improve, but you will actually feel better, too.

The same can be said for stress. While it certainly isn't the single most important factor in bringing that cholesterol level down, every bit helps. And who among us can sincerely argue that a stressful lifestyle leads to good living? We're not asking you to make wholesale changes in your life, but simply to become aware of the stresses that you can control and even eliminate.

Remember that to lower cholesterol and reduce your risk of heart disease we are really talking about a change in lifestyle—a change for the better, through a series of moderate modifications. I hope that using this journal will help give you the impetus to take that all-important first step and to make it a little easier as you experience those first eight weeks of a new, healthier way of living.

SELF-EVALUATION

Date You Begin Your Program: _12/8/02_

TOTAL CHOLESTEROL: 266

LDL: 162 Triglycerides: 125

HDL: 79 Total Cholesterol/HDL: [ ]

CURRENT WEIGHT

125

TARGET WEIGHT

110

See pages 6-8 for more information.

NUTRITION TARGETS

CALORIES PER DAY   FAT PER DAY   CHOLESTEROL PER DAY

1220   27 G

The calorie count is necessary only to compute your fat intake.
See pages 12-13 for more information.

AEROBIC CONDITIONING

RESTING PULSE   TARGET HEART RATE

72   66   80

132/82   *Beginning*   *When conditioned*
         (65% of maximum)   *(80% of maximum)*

See pages 22-24 for more information.

EXERCISE PLANS

2 MILES PER DAY - TREADMILL

AEROBICS - 15 MIN PER DAY

WEIGHTS - 15 MIN PER DAY

SMOKING REDUCTION GOAL: _____
                        (If applicable)

TAKING NIACIN? Yes _____   No __X__
               (If yes, consult your physician first.)

The Diary

FOOD JOURNAL

Time	Food	Fat	Cholesterol

#1: HEART HISTORY

Adults with low incidence of heart disease have an average total cholesterol level between 150 and 200 mg/dl. Remember that total cholesterol levels between 140 and 180 mg/dl are consistently found to be related to the lowest rates of atherosclerosis and coronary heart disease.

FLUIDS

1	2	3	4	5	6	7	8

NIACIN

If you are taking niacin, remember to take your full dosage for the day.

OAT BRAN/SOLUBLE FIBER

| 1 | 2 | 3 |

Meet or exceed your three oat bran muffins, or record other sources of soluble fiber.

Other soluble fiber consumed

EXERCISE

Activity	Time/Repetitions	Pulse Before
		Pulse During
		Weight

STRESS REGISTER

Event/Situation	Proposed Strategy

Successful Strategies:

FOOD JOURNAL

Time	Food	Fat	Cholesterol

#2: A GREAT PAYOFF

Medical authorities state emphatically that a cholesterol reduction of 35%
percent cuts the risk of heart disease in half. Experts at the National Institutes
of Health have put it another way. They have said unequivocally that each
1 percent reduction in blood cholesterol levels produces a 2 percent
reduction in the risk of coronary heart disease.

FLUIDS

1	2	3	4	5	6	7	8

WEEK 1

NIACIN

If you are taking niacin, remember to take your full dosage for the day.

OAT BRAN/SOLUBLE FIBER

| 1 | 2 | 3 |

Meet or exceed your three oat bran muffins, or record other sources of soluble fiber.

Other soluble fiber consumed

EXERCISE

Activity	Time/Repetitions	Pulse Before
		Pulse During
		Weight

STRESS REGISTER

Event/Situation	Proposed Strategy
Successful Strategies:	

FOOD JOURNAL

Time	Food	Fat	Cholesterol

#3: MORE FOR YOUR GRAM

Carbohydrates and proteins contain just 4 calories per gram. There are about 28 grams to an ounce, for those who don't "think metric." But fat, long thought to supply 9 calories per gram, is now believed to contribute as much as 10 to 12 calories per gram! If you just cut down on the amount of fat you eat, you'll automatically and dramatically reduce calories.

FLUIDS

1	2	3	4	5	6	7	8

WEEK 1

NIACIN

If you are taking niacin, remember to take your full dosage for the day.

OAT BRAN/SOLUBLE FIBER

| 1 | 2 | 3 |

Meet or exceed your three oat bran muffins, or record other sources of soluble fiber.

Other soluble fiber consumed

EXERCISE

Activity	Time/Repetitions	Pulse Before
		Pulse During
		Weight

STRESS REGISTER

Event/Situation	Proposed Strategy
Successful Strategies:	

FOOD JOURNAL

Time	Food	Fat	Cholesterol

#4: SUBSTITUTION PRIMER

Here are some helpful tips for substitution in your recipes:
One whole egg = two egg whites   One whole egg = one ounce egg substitute
Cream = evaporated milk   Oil to fry = Pam cooking spray
Butter = soft margarine, corn oil, olive oil, or canola oil
Shortening in baking = substitute one ripe banana for half the shortening

FLUIDS

1	2	3	4	5	6	7	8

WEEK 1

NIACIN

If you are taking niacin, remember to take your full dosage for the day.

OAT BRAN/SOLUBLE FIBER

| 1 | 2 | 3 |

Meet or exceed your three oat bran muffins, or record other sources of soluble fiber.

Other soluble fiber consumed

EXERCISE

Activity	Time/Repetitions	Pulse Before
		Pulse During
		Weight

STRESS REGISTER

Event/Situation	Proposed Strategy
Successful Strategies:	

FOOD JOURNAL

Time	Food	Fat	Cholesterol

#5: CHECK THE LABEL

Remember when reading ingredient labels on foods that ingredients are listed in order of volume. If water is listed first, that means there's more water than anything else. If oat bran is not one of the first ingredients listed, then you are not going to get that much oat bran, regardless of the claims the product makes.

FLUIDS

1	2	3	4	5	6	7	8

NIACIN

If you are taking niacin, remember to
take your full dosage for the day.

OAT BRAN/SOLUBLE FIBER

| 1 | 2 | 3 |

Meet or exceed your three
oat bran muffins, or record
other sources of soluble fiber.

Other soluble fiber consumed

EXERCISE

Activity	Time/Repetitions	Pulse Before
		Pulse During
		Weight

STRESS REGISTER

Event/Situation	Proposed Strategy
Successful Strategies:	

FOOD JOURNAL

Time	Food	Fat	Cholesterol

#6: HEALTHY PIZZA

One delicious low-cholesterol substitute you'll often find in my shopping
cart is Formagg cheese, made by the Galaxy Cheese Company in New Castle,
Pennsylvania. You can use Formagg mozzarella to make your own pizza. While
regular mozzarella has 55 mg of cholesterol per ounce, Formagg has none.
You're also replacing saturated fat with polyunsaturated and monounsaturated fat.

FLUIDS

1	2	3	4	5	6	7	8

NIACIN

If you are taking niacin, remember to
take your full dosage for the day.

OAT BRAN/SOLUBLE FIBER

| 1 | 2 | 3 |

Meet or exceed your three
oat bran muffins, or record
other sources of soluble fiber.

Other soluble fiber consumed

EXERCISE

Activity	Time/Repetitions	Pulse Before
		Pulse During
		Weight

STRESS REGISTER

Event/Situation	Proposed Strategy
Successful Strategies:	

FOOD JOURNAL

Time	Food	Fat	Cholesterol

#7: BEAN BONANZA

Dried beans such as pinto beans, Great Northern beans, lima beans, lentils, red beans and navy beans all contain large amounts of soluble fiber–just like oat bran. In addition to soups and cooked beans, try delicious bean dips such as hummus as a healthful snack.

FLUIDS

| 1 | 2 | 3 | 4 | 5 | 6 | 7 | 8 |

WEEK 1

NIACIN

If you are taking niacin, remember to take your full dosage for the day.

OAT BRAN/SOLUBLE FIBER

| 1 | 2 | 3 |

Meet or exceed your three oat bran muffins, or record other sources of soluble fiber.

Other soluble fiber consumed

EXERCISE

Activity	Time/Repetitions	Pulse Before
		Pulse During
		Weight

STRESS REGISTER

Event/Situation	Proposed Strategy
Successful Strategies:	

FOOD JOURNAL

Time	Food	Fat	Cholesterol

#8: FEEL FULL LONGER

Not only does oat bran help to reduce your cholesterol level, it will also keep you feeling full longer. Oat bran slows down the rate of the so-called gastric emptying, the time it takes for food to move out of the stomach, so you feel full longer.

FLUIDS

1	2	3	4	5	6	7	8

WEEK 2

NIACIN

If you are taking niacin, remember to
take your full dosage for the day.

OAT BRAN/SOLUBLE FIBER

| 1 | 2 | 3 |

Meet or exceed your three
oat bran muffins, or record
other sources of soluble fiber.

_____

_____

Other soluble fiber consumed

EXERCISE

Activity	Time/Repetitions	Pulse Before
		Pulse During
		Weight

STRESS REGISTER

Event/Situation	Proposed Strategy
Successful Strategies:	

FOOD JOURNAL

Time	Food	Fat	Cholesterol

#9: RICE IS NICE

Rice bran is every bit as good as oat bran for lowering cholesterol, if not better.
Only two tablespoons have as much soluble fiber as half a cup of oat bran.
While it isn't quite as versatile in its cooking and baking potential, try sprinkling
it over cereals, as a topping for yogurt, or an ingredient in muffins and other
baked goods.

FLUIDS

1	2	3	4	5	6	7	8

WEEK 2

NIACIN

If you are taking niacin, remember to take your full dosage for the day.

OAT BRAN/SOLUBLE FIBER   [1]   [2]   [3]

Meet or exceed your three
oat bran muffins, or record
other sources of soluble fiber.

Other soluble fiber consumed

EXERCISE

Activity	Time/Repetitions	Pulse Before
		Pulse During
		Weight

STRESS REGISTER

Event/Situation	Proposed Strategy
Successful Strategies:	

FOOD JOURNAL

Time	Food	Fat	Cholesterol

#10: TRAVEL TIP

Although you should not make it an ordinary part of your diet, Metamucil and other laxatives made from psyllium are also rich in soluble fiber and have a cholesterol-lowering effect and can be used as an occasional substitute, such as during travel.

FLUIDS

1	2	3	4	5	6	7	8

WEEK 2

NIACIN

If you are taking niacin, remember to take your full dosage for the day.

OAT BRAN/SOLUBLE FIBER

| 1 | 2 | 3 |

Meet or exceed your three oat bran muffins, or record other sources of soluble fiber.

Other soluble fiber consumed

EXERCISE

Activity	Time/Repetitions	Pulse Before
		Pulse During
		Weight

STRESS REGISTER

Event/Situation	Proposed Strategy
Successful Strategies:	

FOOD JOURNAL

Time	Food	Fat	Cholesterol

#11: FISH POWER

Fish in the diet, at least once and preferably twice a week, will help you in the process of lowering cholesterol, because it contains a special kind of polyunsaturated fat called omega-3 fatty acids. Fish with the highest omega-3 content per gram include, in descending order, sardines, sockeye salmon, and Atlantic mackerel, followed by King salmon, herring, lake trout and other fishes.

FLUIDS

1	2	3	4	5	6	7	8

NIACIN

If you are taking niacin, remember to
take your full dosage for the day.

OAT BRAN/SOLUBLE FIBER

| 1 | 2 | 3 |

Meet or exceed your three
oat bran muffins, or record
other sources of soluble fiber.

Other soluble fiber consumed

EXERCISE

Activity	Time/Repetitions	Pulse Before
		Pulse During
		Weight

STRESS REGISTER

Event/Situation	Proposed Strategy
Successful Strategies:	

FOOD JOURNAL

Time	Food	Fat	Cholesterol

#12: WHICH OIL?

No vegetable oil of any kind has any cholesterol at all, and all vegetable oil is infinitely better than using butter. Most medical authorities suggest using a combination of polyunsaturated oils, like corn oil, and monounsaturated oils, like olive oil. Monounsaturated oils are the ones that protect your HDL, or "good cholesterol" levels.

FLUIDS

1	2	3	4	5	6	7	8

NIACIN

If you are taking niacin, remember to
take your full dosage for the day.

OAT BRAN/SOLUBLE FIBER

| 1 | | 2 | | 3 |

Meet or exceed your three
oat bran muffins, or record
other sources of soluble fiber.

_____

_____
Other soluble fiber consumed

EXERCISE

Activity	Time/Repetitions	Pulse Before
		Pulse During
		Weight

STRESS REGISTER

Event/Situation	Proposed Strategy

Successful Strategies:

FOOD JOURNAL

Time	Food	Fat	Cholesterol

#13: A TOAST TO HEALTH

Remember that moderation should be your byword in alcohol consumption, defined as about 1.5 ounces of alcohol, meaning an average mixed drink or a glass of wine or beer. While a little alcohol may indeed be good for you, there is also evidence that high levels of alcohol consumption has a definite negative effect on heart function.

FLUIDS

1	2	3	4	5	6	7	8

WEEK 2

NIACIN

If you are taking niacin, remember to take your full dosage for the day.

OAT BRAN/SOLUBLE FIBER

| 1 | 2 | 3 |

Meet or exceed your three oat bran muffins, or record other sources of soluble fiber.

Other soluble fiber consumed

EXERCISE

Activity	Time/Repetitions	Pulse Before
		Pulse During
		Weight

STRESS REGISTER

Event/Situation	Proposed Strategy

Successful Strategies:

FOOD JOURNAL

Time	Food	Fat	Cholesterol

#14: SOUP'S ON!

Soup is a wonderful food for people trying to lose weight and is an excellent way to get more vegetables into your diet and a nice alternative to salad. A study done with soup eaters showed that they ate an average of 5 percent fewer calories for the day. Best of all, soups made with beans, lentils, or barley will help lower cholesterol levels. Avoid soups with cream and butter.

FLUIDS

1	2	3	4	5	6	7	8

WEEK 2

NIACIN

If you are taking niacin, remember to
take your full dosage for the day.

OAT BRAN/SOLUBLE FIBER

| 1 | 2 | 3 |

Meet or exceed your three
oat bran muffins, or record
other sources of soluble fiber.

Other soluble fiber consumed

EXERCISE

Activity	Time/Repetitions	Pulse Before
		Pulse During
		Weight

STRESS REGISTER

Event/Situation	Proposed Strategy
Successful Strategies:	

FOOD JOURNAL

Time	Food	Fat	Cholesterol

#15: APPETITE BUSTERS

One oat bran muffin, eaten about twenty minutes before a meal and washed down with a glass of water, will effectively cut down your appetite and you'll eat less food during the meal to come. A piece of fruit or bread can do the same thing.

FLUIDS

1	2	3	4	5	6	7	8

WEEK 3

NIACIN

If you are taking niacin, remember to
take your full dosage for the day.

$\bigcirc$

OAT BRAN/SOLUBLE FIBER

| 1 | 2 | 3 |

Meet or exceed your three
oat bran muffins, or record
other sources of soluble fiber.

Other soluble fiber consumed

EXERCISE

Activity	Time/Repetitions	Pulse Before
		Pulse During
		Weight

STRESS REGISTER

Event/Situation	Proposed Strategy
Successful Strategies:	

FOOD JOURNAL

Time	Food	Fat	Cholesterol

#16: BE FLEXIBLE

Remember, an occasional indulgence is fine-just make up for it in the rest of your diet for the day. It's your choice and the only thing that counts is keeping the total number of grams of fat and milligrams of cholesterol under your own personal limit.

FLUIDS

1	2	3	4	5	6	7	8

NIACIN

If you are taking niacin, remember to take your full dosage for the day.

◯

OAT BRAN/SOLUBLE FIBER

| 1 | 2 | 3 |

Meet or exceed your three oat bran muffins, or record other sources of soluble fiber.

Other soluble fiber consumed

EXERCISE

Activity	Time/Repetitions	Pulse Before
		Pulse During
		Weight

STRESS REGISTER

Event/Situation	Proposed Strategy

Successful Strategies:

FOOD JOURNAL

Time	Food	Fat	Cholesterol

#17: BAKERS BEWARE

Be careful in the bakery. Many or most commercially prepared baked goods
have a high fat and cholesterol content. Choose sourdough and rye bread
and breads that do not contain eggs and shortening. Angel-food cake is one of
the few sweet treats that is made with only egg whites.

FLUIDS

1	2	3	4	5	6	7	8

NIACIN

If you are taking niacin, remember to take your full dosage for the day.

OAT BRAN/SOLUBLE FIBER

| 1 | 2 | 3 |

Meet or exceed your three oat bran muffins, or record other sources of soluble fiber.

Other soluble fiber consumed

EXERCISE

Activity	Time/Repetitions	Pulse Before
		Pulse During
		Weight

STRESS REGISTER

Event/Situation	Proposed Strategy
Successful Strategies:	

FOOD JOURNAL

Time	Food	Fat	Cholesterol

#18: TIMELY EATING

It takes about twenty minutes from the time you eat a morsel of food to the time the body absorbs it into the blood to give that satisfied full feeling. So eat slowly and give yourself time before reaching for that second helping.

FLUIDS

1	2	3	4	5	6	7	8

NIACIN

If you are taking niacin, remember to take your full dosage for the day.

OAT BRAN/SOLUBLE FIBER

| 1 | 2 | 3 |

Meet or exceed your three oat bran muffins, or record other sources of soluble fiber.

Other soluble fiber consumed

EXERCISE

Activity	Time/Repetitions	Pulse Before
		Pulse During
		Weight

STRESS REGISTER

Event/Situation	Proposed Strategy

Successful Strategies:

FOOD JOURNAL

Time	Food	Fat	Cholesterol

#19: LOW-FAT SHELLFISH

Despite what you may have heard, most shellfish, including scallops, Alaskan king crab, clams, oysters and mussels, actually have low cholesterol levels. Only shrimp and lobster have fairly high levels, but each can be eaten in moderate portions without concern. Shellfish are also extremely low in fat.

FLUIDS

1	2	3	4	5	6	7	8

WEEK 3

NIACIN

If you are taking niacin, remember to
take your full dosage for the day.

OAT BRAN/SOLUBLE FIBER   1   2   3

Meet or exceed your three
oat bran muffins, or record
other sources of soluble fiber.

Other soluble fiber consumed

EXERCISE

Activity	Time/Repetitions	Pulse Before
		Pulse During
		Weight

STRESS REGISTER

Event/Situation	Proposed Strategy
Successful Strategies:	

FOOD JOURNAL

Time	Food	Fat	Cholesterol

#20: BETTER THAN BEEF

Try veal as a low-fat alternative to beef. Ground veal contains only about 10 percent fat, while even the leanest ground beef has about 15 percent. You can substitute it in hamburgers, chili or any other recipe calling for ground beef.

FLUIDS

1	2	3	4	5	6	7	8

NIACIN

If you are taking niacin, remember to take your full dosage for the day.

OAT BRAN/SOLUBLE FIBER

| 1 | 2 | 3 |

Meet or exceed your three oat bran muffins, or record other sources of soluble fiber.

Other soluble fiber consumed

EXERCISE

Activity	Time/Repetitions	Pulse Before
		Pulse During
		Weight

STRESS REGISTER

Event/Situation	Proposed Strategy
Successful Strategies:	

FOOD JOURNAL

Time	Food	Fat	Cholesterol

#21: MIXED NUTS

Peanut butter is a definite mixed bag. It is completely cholesterol free, but it does have a large amount of fat–one tablespoon contains more than 7 grams. With 2 or 3 spoonfuls to a typical sandwich, keep this to a once-in-a-while treat. The same applies to nuts in general.

FLUIDS

1	2	3	4	5	6	7	8

WEEK 3

NIACIN

If you are taking niacin, remember to
take your full dosage for the day.

$\bigcirc$

OAT BRAN/SOLUBLE FIBER

| 1 | 2 | 3 |

Meet or exceed your three
oat bran muffins, or record
other sources of soluble fiber.

Other soluble fiber consumed

EXERCISE

Activity	Time/Repetitions	Pulse Before
		Pulse During
		Weight

STRESS REGISTER

Event/Situation	Proposed Strategy
Successful Strategies:	

FOOD JOURNAL

Time	Food	Fat	Cholesterol

#22: LEAN MEAT CONNECTION

The Dakota Lean Meat Company sells cuts of beef that contain as little as 1.2 percent fat. Dakota offers New York strip, ribeye, sirloin and hamburger – all with a fraction of the fat normally found in similar cuts. Since the meat is lean, remember to reduce the cooking time. See The Shopping List for ordering details.

FLUIDS

1	2	3	4	5	6	7	8

NIACIN

If you are taking niacin, remember to
take your full dosage for the day.

$\bigcirc$

OAT BRAN/SOLUBLE FIBER

| 1 | 2 | 3 |

Meet or exceed your three
oat bran muffins, or record
other sources of soluble fiber.

Other soluble fiber consumed

EXERCISE

Activity	Time/Repetitions	Pulse Before
		Pulse During
		Weight

STRESS REGISTER

Event/Situation	Proposed Strategy
Successful Strategies:	

FOOD JOURNAL

Time	Food	Fat	Cholesterol

#23: PARMESAN PLEASURE

Using grated Parmesan is one nice way to get the flavor of cheese in your foods without the fat. One tablespoon has only 1.5 grams of fat, while a one-ounce portion of hard Parmesan has 7.3 grams.

FLUIDS

1	2	3	4	5	6	7	8

NIACIN

If you are taking niacin, remember to
take your full dosage for the day.

OAT BRAN/SOLUBLE FIBER

| 1 | 2 | 3 |

Meet or exceed your three
oat bran muffins, or record
other sources of soluble fiber.

Other soluble fiber consumed

EXERCISE

Activity	Time/Repetitions	Pulse Before
		Pulse During
		Weight

STRESS REGISTER

Event/Situation	Proposed Strategy
Successful Strategies:	

FOOD JOURNAL

Time	Food	Fat	Cholesterol

#24: TEMPTING TURKEY

Turkey breast has a mere trace of fat, less than 4 percent. Dark meat has more than 8 percent, while skin contains more than 39 percent fat. The same applies to chicken-it's a good source of protein without a lot of fat and cholesterol, and the breast is best.

FLUIDS

1	2	3	4	5	6	7	8

NIACIN

If you are taking niacin, remember to take your full dosage for the day.

OAT BRAN/SOLUBLE FIBER

| 1 | 2 | 3 |

Meet or exceed your three oat bran muffins, or record other sources of soluble fiber.

Other soluble fiber consumed

EXERCISE

Activity	Time/Repetitions	Pulse Before
		Pulse During
		Weight

STRESS REGISTER

Event/Situation	Proposed Strategy
Successful Strategies:	

FOOD JOURNAL

Time	Food	Fat	Cholesterol

#25: NOT ALL YOGURTS ARE EQUAL

Check the label carefully on yogurts–they're not all the same. Nonfat brands have .4 gram of fat, the more common low-fat has about 3.4 grams, and whole-milk types can have 7.7 grams per eight-ounce container or more. Alta Dena and Yoplait are two European-style custard yogurts with none of the fat usually found in such "premium" yogurts.

FLUIDS

| 1 | 2 | 3 | 4 | 5 | 6 | 7 | 8 |

WEEK 4

NIACIN

If you are taking niacin, remember to
take your full dosage for the day.

$\bigcirc$

OAT BRAN/SOLUBLE FIBER

| 1 | 2 | 3 |

Meet or exceed your three
oat bran muffins, or record
other sources of soluble fiber.

_____

_____
Other soluble fiber consumed

EXERCISE

Activity	Time/Repetitions	Pulse Before
		Pulse During
		Weight

STRESS REGISTER

Event/Situation	Proposed Strategy
Successful Strategies:	

FOOD JOURNAL

Time	Food	Fat	Cholesterol

#26: ALL-AMERICAN DANGER

Look out for salami–just one slice has 9 to 12 grams of fat. But one slice of Canadian bacon has only 2 grams. The all-American hot dog is unfortunately another source of excessive fat in the diet. An all-beef Oscar Meyer frankfurter has 13.5 grams of fat.

FLUIDS

1	2	3	4	5	6	7	8

WEEK 4

NIACIN

If you are taking niacin, remember to
take your full dosage for the day.

$\bigcirc$

OAT BRAN/SOLUBLE FIBER

| 1 | 2 | 3 |

Meet or exceed your three
oat bran muffins, or record
other sources of soluble fiber.

Other soluble fiber consumed

EXERCISE

Activity	Time/Repetitions	Pulse Before
		Pulse During
		Weight

STRESS REGISTER

Event/Situation	Proposed Strategy
Successful Strategies:	

FOOD JOURNAL

Time	Food	Fat	Cholesterol

#27: THE "NATURAL TRAP"

Advertisers have convinced the buying public that granola bars are a healthful, nutritious "natural" snack. A closer look shows them to be no more than candy bars in disguise, loaded with fat and sugar.

FLUIDS

1	2	3	4	5	6	7	8

WEEK 4

NIACIN

If you are taking niacin, remember to
take your full dosage for the day.

OAT BRAN/SOLUBLE FIBER

| 1 | 2 | 3 |

Meet or exceed your three
oat bran muffins, or record
other sources of soluble fiber.

Other soluble fiber consumed

EXERCISE

Activity	Time/Repetitions	Pulse Before
		Pulse During
		Weight

STRESS REGISTER

Event/Situation	Proposed Strategy
Successful Strategies:	

FOOD JOURNAL

Time	Food	Fat	Cholesterol

#28: PORTION CONTROL

You can keep eating your favorite meats, as long as you keep the portion size under control. An adequate portion should consist of 3.5 to 4 grams of beef or chicken, and never more than 5 to 6 ounces. When you buy by the pound, make it easy on yourself and split the meat into four equal portions before you even cook it.

FLUIDS

1	2	3	4	5	6	7	8

WEEK 4

NIACIN

If you are taking niacin, remember to take your full dosage for the day.

$\bigcirc$

OAT BRAN/SOLUBLE FIBER

| 1 | 2 | 3 |

Meet or exceed your three oat bran muffins, or record other sources of soluble fiber.

_____

_____
Other soluble fiber consumed

EXERCISE

Activity	Time/Repetitions	Pulse Before
		Pulse During
		Weight

STRESS REGISTER

Event/Situation	Proposed Strategy
Successful Strategies:	

FOOD JOURNAL

Time	Food	Fat	Cholesterol

#29: BETTER THAN BUTTER

A terrific way to cut down on fats is a product called Butter Buds. These packets of powder really do have the flavor of butter, with no fat or cholesterol. Similar products include Molly McButter and O'Butter.

FLUIDS

1	2	3	4	5	6	7	8

NIACIN

If you are taking niacin, remember to
take your full dosage for the day.

OAT BRAN/SOLUBLE FIBER

| 1 | 2 | 3 |

Meet or exceed your three
oat bran muffins, or record
other sources of soluble fiber.

Other soluble fiber consumed

EXERCISE

Activity	Time/Repetitions	Pulse Before
		Pulse During
		Weight

STRESS REGISTER

Event/Situation	Proposed Strategy
Successful Strategies:	

FOOD JOURNAL

Time	Food	Fat	Cholesterol

#30: SAFE CHEESE

Although regular cheese has a lot of fat and should be avoided, today you can easily choose from a number of filled cheeses, in which the butterfat has been replaced with soybean or other vegetable oil. My personal preference is Formagg, made by the Galaxy Cheese Company.

FLUIDS

1	2	3	4	5	6	7	8

NIACIN

If you are taking niacin, remember to
take your full dosage for the day.

OAT BRAN/SOLUBLE FIBER

Meet or exceed your three
oat bran muffins, or record
other sources of soluble fiber.

Other soluble fiber consumed

EXERCISE

Activity	Time/Repetitions	Pulse Before
		Pulse During
		Weight

STRESS REGISTER

Event/Situation	Proposed Strategy
Successful Strategies:	

FOOD JOURNAL

Time	Food	Fat	Cholesterol

#31: KNOW YOUR FIBER

Insoluble fiber, the type found in fruits and vegetables, is the fiber that moves food more quickly through the digestive tract. Soluble fiber, found in foods like oat bran and rice bran, actively helps to lower cholesterol.

FLUIDS

1	2	3	4	5	6	7	8

WEEK 5

NIACIN

If you are taking niacin, remember to
take your full dosage for the day.

OAT BRAN/SOLUBLE FIBER   [1]   [2]   [3]

Meet or exceed your three
oat bran muffins, or record
other sources of soluble fiber.

Other soluble fiber consumed

EXERCISE

Activity	Time/Repetitions	Pulse Before
		Pulse During
		Weight

STRESS REGISTER

Event/Situation	Proposed Strategy
Successful Strategies:	

FOOD JOURNAL

Time	Food	Fat	Cholesterol

#32: SODIUM ALERT

The average American unquestionably consumes an excessive amount of salt and other forms of sodium. About 10 percent of the population has high blood pressure and is directly at risk in proportion to the amount of sodium consumed. In any case, reduced sodium in your diet is a good idea.

FLUIDS

1	2	3	4	5	6	7	8

WEEK 5

NIACIN

If you are taking niacin, remember to
take your full dosage for the day.

$\bigcirc$

OAT BRAN/SOLUBLE FIBER

| 1 | 2 | 3 |

Meet or exceed your three
oat bran muffins, or record
other sources of soluble fiber.

Other soluble fiber consumed

EXERCISE

Activity	Time/Repetitions	Pulse Before
		Pulse During
		Weight

STRESS REGISTER

Event/Situation	Proposed Strategy
Successful Strategies:	

FOOD JOURNAL

Time	Food	Fat	Cholesterol

#33: THE MYSTERIES OF BARLEY

While barley contains much less soluble fiber per gram than oat bran, it seems to have a capacity for cholesterol reduction far beyond what its soluble fiber content would predict. Scientists are now at work trying to figure out just what it is about barley that makes it effective.

FLUIDS

1	2	3	4	5	6	7	8

WEEK 5

NIACIN

If you are taking niacin, remember to
take your full dosage for the day.

$\bigcirc$

OAT BRAN/SOLUBLE FIBER

| 1 | | 2 | | 3 |

Meet or exceed your three
oat bran muffins, or record
other sources of soluble fiber.

_____

_____
Other soluble fiber consumed

EXERCISE

Activity	Time/Repetitions	Pulse Before
		Pulse During
		Weight

STRESS REGISTER

Event/Situation	Proposed Strategy
Successful Strategies:	

FOOD JOURNAL

Time	Food	Fat	Cholesterol

#34: FISH OR FOUL?

While most fish and shellfish are an excellent part of any cholesterol-lowering diet, there are a few seafood dishes one must be careful about eating on a regular basis, notably caviar, squid, and abalone, all of which are quite high in cholesterol.

FLUIDS

| 1 | 2 | 3 | 4 | 5 | 6 | 7 | 8 |

NIACIN

If you are taking niacin, remember to take your full dosage for the day.

$\bigcirc$

OAT BRAN/SOLUBLE FIBER

| 1 | 2 | 3 |

Meet or exceed your three oat bran muffins, or record other sources of soluble fiber.

Other soluble fiber consumed

EXERCISE

Activity	Time/Repetitions	Pulse Before
		Pulse During
		Weight

STRESS REGISTER

Event/Situation	Proposed Strategy
Successful Strategies:	

FOOD JOURNAL

Time	Food	Fat	Cholesterol

#35: AN APPLE A DAY . . .

Another wonderful alternative to oat bran is apple fiber, which has a little more than 3 grams of soluble fiber per ounce–even higher than oat bran. Look for Tastee Apple Fiber and Hearty Life Apple Fiber in supermarkets, or Sovex Apple Fiber in health-food stores. You can use it in baking muffins and cookies and as an added ingredient in tomato sauce for a thicker, slightly sweet sauce.

FLUIDS

1	2	3	4	5	6	7	8

WEEK 5

NIACIN

If you are taking niacin, remember to
take your full dosage for the day.

OAT BRAN/SOLUBLE FIBER

| 1 | 2 | 3 |

Meet or exceed your three
oat bran muffins, or record
other sources of soluble fiber.

Other soluble fiber consumed

EXERCISE

Activity	Time/Repetitions	Pulse Before
	'	
		Pulse During
		Weight

STRESS REGISTER

Event/Situation	Proposed Strategy
Successful Strategies:	

FOOD JOURNAL

Time	Food	Fat	Cholesterol

#36: CREAMY IDEAS

For a healthy coffee creamer, try using nonfat dry milk powder spooned in the same way you would use nondairy creamers. Or try evaporated skim milk in cans, which has a rich taste and can be substituted in any recipe calling for cream.

FLUIDS

1	2	3	4	5	6	7	8

NIACIN

If you are taking niacin, remember to
take your full dosage for the day.

OAT BRAN/SOLUBLE FIBER

| 1 | 2 | 3 |

Meet or exceed your three
oat bran muffins, or record
other sources of soluble fiber.

Other soluble fiber consumed

EXERCISE

Activity	Time/Repetitions	Pulse Before
		Pulse During
		Weight

STRESS REGISTER

Event/Situation	Proposed Strategy
Successful Strategies:	

FOOD JOURNAL

Time	Food	Fat	Cholesterol

#37: FIBER YOU CAN DRINK

Guar gum is another type of soluble fiber that until recently was impractical
in real-life eating. You can now find it in capsules and powder, to be consumed
in a beverage mixed with water or incorporated into a variety of shake recipes.
Based on the research to date, a total of 15 grams, or one teaspoonful three times
daily, would be expected to yield a considerable benefit.

FLUIDS

1	2	3	4	5	6	7	8

WEEK 6

NIACIN

If you are taking niacin, remember to
take your full dosage for the day.

$\bigcirc$

OAT BRAN/SOLUBLE FIBER

| 1 | 2 | 3 |

Meet or exceed your three
oat bran muffins, or record
other sources of soluble fiber.

Other soluble fiber consumed

EXERCISE

Activity	Time/Repetitions	Pulse Before
		Pulse During
		Weight

STRESS REGISTER

Event/Situation	Proposed Strategy
Successful Strategies:	

FOOD JOURNAL

Time	Food	Fat	Cholesterol

#38: THE WAY TO LEAN

For ground beef that's as low as 5 percent fat, select a London broil, top round steak or other very lean cut. Ask your butcher to trim off all the visible fat, even if it means cutting into the meat a bit, and then grind it.

FLUIDS

1	2	3	4	5	6	7	8

WEEK 6

NIACIN

If you are taking niacin, remember to
take your full dosage for the day.

OAT BRAN/SOLUBLE FIBER

| 1 | 2 | 3 |

Meet or exceed your three
oat bran muffins, or record
other sources of soluble fiber.

Other soluble fiber consumed

EXERCISE

Activity	Time/Repetitions	Pulse Before
		Pulse During
		Weight

STRESS REGISTER

Event/Situation	Proposed Strategy
Successful Strategies:	

FOOD JOURNAL

Time	Food	Fat	Cholesterol

#39: HEALTHY FRYING

There is a company called Pacific Rice Products (916) 662-5056 that now markets rice-bran oil, an excellent replacement for cooking oil that will reduce your cholesterol. You can use it for everything from wok stir-frying to french fries.

FLUIDS

| 1 | 2 | 3 | 4 | 5 | 6 | 7 | 8 |

WEEK 6

NIACIN

If you are taking niacin, remember to
take your full dosage for the day.

OAT BRAN/SOLUBLE FIBER

| 1 | 2 | 3 |

Meet or exceed your three
oat bran muffins, or record
other sources of soluble fiber.

Other soluble fiber consumed

EXERCISE

Activity	Time/Repetitions	Pulse Before
		Pulse During
		Weight

STRESS REGISTER

Event/Situation	Proposed Strategy
Successful Strategies:	

FOOD JOURNAL

Time	Food	Fat	Cholesterol

#40: HAM IT UP

Most pork tends to have a hefty dollop of fat but the remarkable exception is ham. You can enjoy dinners of ham steaks, ham sandwiches, or breakfasts of ham or Canadian bacon, all of which is extremely low in fat. Just check the labels carefully and select the ham products with very low fat content.

FLUIDS

1	2	3	4	5	6	7	8

WEEK 6

NIACIN

If you are taking niacin, remember to
take your full dosage for the day.

OAT BRAN/SOLUBLE FIBER

| 1 | 2 | 3 |

Meet or exceed your three
oat bran muffins, or record
other sources of soluble fiber.

Other soluble fiber consumed

EXERCISE

Activity	Time/Repetitions	Pulse Before
		Pulse During
		Weight

STRESS REGISTER

Event/Situation	Proposed Strategy

Successful Strategies:

FOOD JOURNAL

Time	Food	Fat	Cholesterol

#41: NOODLE NEWS

Until recently egg noodles have presented a problem because of their cholesterol content. But a new product, No Yolks, is a cholesterol-free noodle made with durum flour, corn flour and egg whites, and they are delicious. If you can't find them in your store, see The Shopping List for details.

FLUIDS

1	2	3	4	5	6	7	8

NIACIN

If you are taking niacin, remember to
take your full dosage for the day.

OAT BRAN/SOLUBLE FIBER

| 1 | 2 | 3 |

Meet or exceed your three
oat bran muffins, or record
other sources of soluble fiber.

Other soluble fiber consumed

EXERCISE

Activity	Time/Repetitions	Pulse Before
		Pulse During
		Weight

STRESS REGISTER

Event/Situation	Proposed Strategy
Successful Strategies:	

FOOD JOURNAL

Time	Food	Fat	Cholesterol

#42: TIME FOR NIACIN

Since I first began to use niacin, scientists have learned that the body makes most of its cholesterol in the evening and nighttime hours. It's best to take your niacin late in the day–ideally, at lunch, dinner and bedtime. A tablet in the morning with breakfast would have the least effect. Do not take more than one tablet at a time.

FLUIDS

1	2	3	4	5	6	7	8

NIACIN

If you are taking niacin, remember to
take your full dosage for the day.

OAT BRAN/SOLUBLE FIBER

| 1 | 2 | 3 |

Meet or exceed your three
oat bran muffins, or record
other sources of soluble fiber.

Other soluble fiber consumed

EXERCISE

Activity	Time/Repetitions	Pulse Before
		Pulse During
		Weight

STRESS REGISTER

Event/Situation	Proposed Strategy
Successful Strategies:	

FOOD JOURNAL

Time	Food	Fat	Cholesterol

#43: SAVE YOUR LIVER

Niacin is metabolized by the liver, the same organ that breaks down alcohol. If you are taking niacin as part of your program, keep your alcohol consumption under control; otherwise you'll be asking your liver to do double duty.

FLUIDS

1	2	3	4	5	6	7	8

NIACIN

If you are taking niacin, remember to
take your full dosage for the day.

OAT BRAN/SOLUBLE FIBER

| 1 | 2 | 3 |

Meet or exceed your three
oat bran muffins, or record
other sources of soluble fiber.

Other soluble fiber consumed

EXERCISE

Activity	Time/Repetitions	Pulse Before
		Pulse During
		Weight

STRESS REGISTER

Event/Situation	Proposed Strategy
Successful Strategies:	

FOOD JOURNAL

Time	Food	Fat	Cholesterol

#44: GRADE-A SUBSTITUTE

For a delicious version of scrambled eggs, use a combination of fresh egg whites and Egg Beaters. The fresh whites provide a flavorful perk, and you may not be able to tell the difference from whole eggs. I strongly recommend Egg Beaters since no oil is added, unlike other egg substitutes.

FLUIDS

1	2	3	4	5	6	7	8

WEEK 7

NIACIN

If you are taking niacin, remember to
take your full dosage for the day.

OAT BRAN/SOLUBLE FIBER | 1 | 2 | 3 |

Meet or exceed your three
oat bran muffins, or record
other sources of soluble fiber.

Other soluble fiber consumed

EXERCISE

Activity	Time/Repetitions	Pulse Before
		Pulse During
		Weight

STRESS REGISTER

Event/Situation	Proposed Strategy
Successful Strategies:	

FOOD JOURNAL

Time	Food	Fat	Cholesterol

#45: NEARLY NUTS

A delicious low-fat alternative for those of us who love the crunch of nuts is chestnuts. They taste great when roasted in the shell and contain only .1 gram of fat each. Just score and pop them into the oven at 350 degrees for an hour.

FLUIDS

1	2	3	4	5	6	7	8

WEEK 7

NIACIN

If you are taking niacin, remember to
take your full dosage for the day.

$\bigcirc$

OAT BRAN/SOLUBLE FIBER

| 1 | 2 | 3 |

Meet or exceed your three
oat bran muffins, or record
other sources of soluble fiber.

Other soluble fiber consumed

EXERCISE

Activity	Time/Repetitions	Pulse Before
		Pulse During
		Weight

STRESS REGISTER

Event/Situation	Proposed Strategy
Successful Strategies:	

FOOD JOURNAL

Time	Food	Fat	Cholesterol

#46: SWEET TREATS

For special treats, Sweet Deceit is a company that makes all sorts of sinful goodies without the sin. While expensive, their assorted cakes have just 4 to 5 grams of fat per 3 1/2 ounce serving. The whole line is available by mail-order; see The Shopping List for details.

FLUIDS

1	2	3	4	5	6	7	8

NIACIN

If you are taking niacin, remember to
take your full dosage for the day.

$\bigcirc$

OAT BRAN/SOLUBLE FIBER

| 1 | 2 | 3 |

Meet or exceed your three
oat bran muffins, or record
other sources of soluble fiber.

Other soluble fiber consumed

EXERCISE

Activity	Time/Repetitions	Pulse Before
		Pulse During
		Weight

STRESS REGISTER

Event/Situation	Proposed Strategy
Successful Strategies:	

FOOD JOURNAL

Time	Food	Fat	Cholesterol

#47: BRAN NEWS

When I first wrote *The 8-Week Cholesterol Cure*, oat bran was *the* source of soluble fiber. Then we learned more about dried beans and peas. Next it was pectin from apple fiber. Now we have rice bran. And work continues on bran of other cereals. Watch, especially, for corn bran to be available soon, and barley bran may reach the market shortly.

FLUIDS

1	2	3	4	5	6	7	8

NIACIN

If you are taking niacin, remember to
take your full dosage for the day.

OAT BRAN/SOLUBLE FIBER

| 1 | 2 | 3 |

Meet or exceed your three
oat bran muffins, or record
other sources of soluble fiber.

Other soluble fiber consumed

EXERCISE

Activity	Time/Repetitions	Pulse Before
		Pulse During
	•	
		Weight

STRESS REGISTER

Event/Situation	Proposed Strategy
Successful Strategies:	

FOOD JOURNAL

Time	Food	Fat	Cholesterol

#48: WHAT LEAN MEANS

Meat and poultry labelled "lean" must contain no more than 10 percent fat by weight, according to new USDA regulations. "Extra lean" means no more than 5 percent fat. "Leaner" means the product has at least 25 percent less fat than the regular product. In all cases, the actual fat content will be listed.

FLUIDS

1	2	3	4	5	6	7	8

WEEK 7

NIACIN

If you are taking niacin, remember to
take your full dosage for the day.

$\bigcirc$

OAT BRAN/SOLUBLE FIBER

| 1 | 2 | 3 |

Meet or exceed your three
oat bran muffins, or record
other sources of soluble fiber.

Other soluble fiber consumed

EXERCISE

Activity	Time/Repetitions	Pulse Before
		Pulse During
		Weight

STRESS REGISTER

Event/Situation	Proposed Strategy
Successful Strategies:	

FOOD JOURNAL

Time	Food	Fat	Cholesterol

#49: FAT FACTS

The recommendation today is to strictly limit saturated fats, replacing them with monounsaturated and some polyunsaturated fats. Saturated fats come from animal fats in meat, dairy products and shortening, plus tropical oils, including coconut, palm and palm kernel oils.

FLUIDS

1	2	3	4	5	6	7	8

NIACIN

If you are taking niacin, remember to take your full dosage for the day.

◯

OAT BRAN/SOLUBLE FIBER

| 1 | 2 | 3 |

Meet or exceed your three oat bran muffins, or record other sources of soluble fiber.

Other soluble fiber consumed

EXERCISE

Activity	Time/Repetitions	Pulse Before
		Pulse During
		Weight

STRESS REGISTER

Event/Situation	Proposed Strategy

Successful Strategies:

FOOD JOURNAL

Time	Food	Fat	Cholesterol

#50: WHAT'S IN A NAME?

"Cholesterol-free" means the product has less than 2 milligrams of cholesterol per serving. "Low-cholesterol" means the food contains less than 20 milligrams per serving. "Cholesterol-reduced" implies that the food contains 75 percent less cholesterol than a comparable product.

FLUIDS

1	2	3	4	5	6	7	8

NIACIN

If you are taking niacin, remember to
take your full dosage for the day.

OAT BRAN/SOLUBLE FIBER

| 1 | 2 | 3 |

Meet or exceed your three
oat bran muffins, or record
other sources of soluble fiber.

Other soluble fiber consumed

EXERCISE

Activity	Time/Repetitions	Pulse Before
		Pulse During
		Weight

STRESS REGISTER

Event/Situation	Proposed Strategy
Successful Strategies:	

FOOD JOURNAL

Time	Food	Fat	Cholesterol

#51: *MONOS AND POLYS*

While monounsaturated fats are favored because they do the best job of protecting HDL levels, you still don't want to have too much fat in your diet. Monounsaturated fats include olives and olive oils, peanuts and peanut oil, avocados, cashews, and canola oil (Puritan and others). Polyunsaturated fats include vegetable oils, including corn oil, soybean oil, safflower oil, and others.

FLUIDS

1	2	3	4	5	6	7	8

NIACIN

If you are taking niacin, remember to
take your full dosage for the day.

⬭

OAT BRAN/SOLUBLE FIBER

| 1 | 2 | 3 |

Meet or exceed your three
oat bran muffins, or record
other sources of soluble fiber.

Other soluble fiber consumed

EXERCISE

Activity	Time/Repetitions	Pulse Before
		Pulse During
		Weight

STRESS REGISTER

Event/Situation	Proposed Strategy
Successful Strategies:	

FOOD JOURNAL

Time	Food	Fat	Cholesterol

#52: SAD DECEPTION

One unfortunate side effect of people's concerns about their cholesterol is the growing amount of quackery that preys on these concerns. There is no clinical evidence that evening primrose drops total cholesterol levels or that lecithin melts cholesterol away. Chelation therapy is a total fraud. Don't be fooled; check with your doctor before trying new treatments.

FLUIDS

1	2	3	4	5	6	7	8

NIACIN

If you are taking niacin, remember to
take your full dosage for the day.

$\bigcirc$

OAT BRAN/SOLUBLE FIBER

| 1 | 2 | 3 |

Meet or exceed your three
oat bran muffins, or record
other sources of soluble fiber.

Other soluble fiber consumed

EXERCISE

Activity	Time/Repetitions	Pulse Before
		Pulse During
		Weight

STRESS REGISTER

Event/Situation	Proposed Strategy
Successful Strategies:	

FOOD JOURNAL

Time	Food	Fat	Cholesterol

#53: NOT JUST FOR MEN

Many people think that only men are at risk of heart disease, but it is also
the number one killer of American females–killing seven times more women
than breast cancer does. Yet women do tend to have offsetting high levels of
protective HDL, so make sure that your doctor does a full analysis before starting
a cholesterol-lowering program.

FLUIDS

1	2	3	4	5	6	7	8

NIACIN

If you are taking niacin, remember to
take your full dosage for the day.

◯

OAT BRAN/SOLUBLE FIBER

| 1 | 2 | 3 |

Meet or exceed your three
oat bran muffins, or record
other sources of soluble fiber.

Other soluble fiber consumed

EXERCISE

Activity	Time/Repetitions	Pulse Before
		Pulse During
		Weight

STRESS REGISTER

Event/Situation	Proposed Strategy

Successful Strategies:

FOOD JOURNAL

Time	Food	Fat	Cholesterol

#54: THE NEXT GENERATION

Many of our chlidren also have elevated cholesterol levels, placing them at future risk of heart disease. The best time to test children is when they reach school age. Their cholesterol levels are lower than adults' and ideally should be in the 140 to 160 mg/dl range. Just as you warn your children about other dangers, stress the positive aspects of a good diet.

FLUIDS

1	2	3	4	5	6	7	8

NIACIN

If you are taking niacin, remember to
take your full dosage for the day.

OAT BRAN/SOLUBLE FIBER

| 1 | 2 | 3 |

Meet or exceed your three
oat bran muffins, or record
other sources of soluble fiber.

Other soluble fiber consumed

EXERCISE

Activity	Time/Repetitions	Pulse Before
		Pulse During
		Weight

STRESS REGISTER

Event/Situation	Proposed Strategy
Successful Strategies:	

FOOD JOURNAL

Time	Food	Fat	Cholesterol

#55: NEVER TOO LATE

It's never too late to start a lifestyle of heart disease prevention. Actually, the greatest occurrence of heart disease, heart attacks and coronary bypass surgery is in those over sixty-five. High cholesterol levels are a risk factor for older folks as much as for their sons and daughters, and those numbers can come down safely and effectively through this program.

FLUIDS

1	2	3	4	5	6	7	8

WEEK 8

NIACIN

If you are taking niacin, remember to
take your full dosage for the day.

$\bigcirc$

OAT BRAN/SOLUBLE FIBER

| 1 | 2 | 3 |

Meet or exceed your three
oat bran muffins, or record
other sources of soluble fiber.

Other soluble fiber consumed

EXERCISE

Activity	Time/Repetitions	Pulse Before
		Pulse During
		Weight

STRESS REGISTER

Event/Situation	Proposed Strategy
Successful Strategies:	

FOOD JOURNAL

Time	Food	Fat	Cholesterol

#56: TEST TIME

Everyone taking niacin as part of this program should have a liver function test done two to three months after initiating niacin therapy and once a year thereafter. If you've been using niacin, now is the time for you to make an appointment with your doctor to have this test done as part of your cholesterol evaluation.

FLUIDS

1	2	3	4	5	6	7	8

NIACIN

If you are taking niacin, remember to take your full dosage for the day.

OAT BRAN/SOLUBLE FIBER

| 1 | 2 | 3 |

Meet or exceed your three oat bran muffins, or record other sources of soluble fiber.

_____

_____

Other soluble fiber consumed

EXERCISE

Activity	Time/Repetitions	Pulse Before
		Pulse During
		Weight

STRESS REGISTER

Event/Situation	Proposed Strategy

Successful Strategies:

SELF-EVALUATION

TOTAL CHOLESTEROL: [ ]

LDL: [ ]   Triglycerides: [ ]

HDL: [ ]   Total Cholesterol/HDL: [ ]

CURRENT WEIGHT	TARGET WEIGHT	WEIGHT LOST
[ ]	[ ]	[ ]

NUTRITION TARGETS

FAT PER DAY	CHOLESTEROL PER DAY
[ ]	[ ]

Remember to maintain your new diet. The 8-Week program is just the beginning of a whole new way of living.

AEROBIC CONDITIONING

RESTING PULSE	TARGET HEART RATE
[ ]	[ ]

(65–80% of maximum)

Now that you are in shape, you still need aerobic exercise three or four times a week just to maintain your conditioning.

EXERCISE ROUTINE

_____

_____

_____

SMOKING REDUCTION GOAL: _____

(If applicable)

The Food Counter
Calorie, Fat, Cholesterol and Sodium Content of Foods

FOOD	SERVING SIZE	CALORIES	FAT (grams)	CHOLESTEROL (mgs)	SODIUM (mgs)
Carnation Breakfast Bar	1 bar	210	11.0	1	140-220
Milk chocolate bar or 6-7 kisses	1 oz.	150	9.2	5	7
Milk chocolate with almonds	1 oz.	155	9.3	4	22

CHEESE

FOOD	SERVING SIZE	CALORIES	FAT (grams)	CHOLESTEROL (mgs)	SODIUM (mgs)
American	1 oz.	105	8.4	27	318
Formagg American	1/2 cup	70	5.0	0	230
Blue	1 oz.	103	8.5	21	390
Brick	1 oz.	103	8.5	25	157
Brie	1 oz.	94	7.8	28	176
Camembert	1 oz.	84	6.9	20	236
Cheddar	1 oz.	112	9.1	30	197
Formagg Cheddar	1 oz.	70	5.0	0	140
Colby	1 oz.	110	9.0	27	169
Cottage (1% fat)	1/2 cup	82	1.6	5	460
Cottage (2% fat)	1/2 cup	100	2.2	9	460
Cottage (4% fat)	1/2 cup	120	4.7	12	460
Cream cheese	2 tbsp.	99	9.9	34	84
Formagg Cream cheese	1 oz.	80	7.0	0	70
Edam	1 oz.	87	5.7	25	270
Feta	1 oz.	74	6.0	25	312
Gouda	1 oz.	100	7.7	32	229
Gruyere	1 oz.	115	8.9	31	94
Monterey Jack	1 oz.	105	8.5	30	150
Formagg Monterey Jack	1 oz.	70	5.0	0	140
Mozzarella	1 oz.	79	6.1	22	104
Mozzarella (part skim)	1 oz.	78	4.8	15	148
Formagg Mozzarella	1 oz.	70	5.0	0	140
Muenster	1 oz.	104	8.5	27	178
Neufchatel	1 oz..	73	6.6	21	112
Parmesan (grated)	1 tbsp.	23	1.5	4	93
Parmesan (hard)	1 oz.	111	7.3	19	454
Formagg Parmesan (shredded)	1 oz.	70	4.0	0	400
Provolone	1 oz.	98	7.3	19	245
Formagg Provolone	1 oz.	70	5.0	0	140

FOOD	SERVING SIZE	CALORIES	FAT (grams)	CHOLESTEROL (mgs)	SODIUM (mgs)
Ricotta (13% fat)	1/2 cup	216	16.1	63	104
Ricotta (8% fat)	1/2 cup	171	9.8	40	155
Formagg Ricotta	4 oz.	130	5.0	0	40
Romano	1 oz.	110	7.6	29	340
Roquefort	1 oz.	105	8.7	26	513
Swiss (pasteurized processed)	1 oz.	95	7.1	26	388
Formagg Swiss	1 oz.	70	5.0	0	140
Cheezola	1 oz.	89	6.4	1	448
Countdown	1 oz.	39	0.3	1	434
Lite Line	1 oz.	50	2.0	10	410
Light n' Lively	1 oz.	70	4.0	15	350+
Cheez Whiz spread	1 oz.	80	6.0	15	490
Lo-Chol	1 oz.	105	9.0	4	130
Cheddamelt	1 oz.	80	6.0	5	310
Pizza-Mate	1 oz.	90	7.0	5	NA

COMBINATION FOODS

FOOD	SERVING SIZE	CALORIES	FAT (grams)	CHOLESTEROL (mgs)	SODIUM (mgs)
Beefaroni	7 oz.	229	7.9	50	1044
Beef pot pie	1 pie	443	25.4	41	1008
Beef stew	1 cup	186	7.3	33	966
Chicken & noodles	6 oz.	151	4.9	20	816
Dennison's Chili con Carne	16-oz. can	320	17.0	30	10
Egg roll	1/2 oz.	210+	6.7+	12+	530+
Morton Salisbury Steak Dinner	1 oz.	373	15.6	47	1213
Franco-American Macaroni and Cheese	1 cup	180	8.0	26	900
ARMOUR CLASSIC LITE DINNERS:					
Beef Pepper Steak	1	270	9.0	55	900
Chicken Burgundy	1	230	4.0	75	920
Chicken Oriental	1	240	4.0	75	730
Fillet of Cod Divan	1	280	7.0	80	990
Chicken Breast Marsala	1	270	7.0	NA	NA
Seafood, Natural Herbs	1	240	5.0	25	1440
Sliced Beef with Broccoli	1	280	7.0	70	2140
Turf n Surf	1	260	8.0	105	690
Turkey Parmesan	1	260	7.0	75	960

FOOD	SERVING SIZE	CALORIES	FAT (grams)	CHOLESTEROL (mgs)	SODIUM (mgs)
Veal Pepper Steak	1	280	8.0	90	480
LEAN CUISINE: (Stouffer's)					
Cheese Cannelloni	1	270	10.0	45	950
Chicken & Vegetables with Vermicelli	1	260	7.0	40	1250
Chicken Chow Mein	1	250	5.0	25	1160
Fillet of Fish Florentine	1	240	9.0	100	800
Glazed Chicken	1	270	8.0	55	840
Linguini/Clam	1	260	7.0	40	860
Meatball Stew	1	250	9.0	65	1165
Oriental Beef	1	260	8.0	35	1270
Oriental Scallops	1	220	3.0	20	1200
Spaghetti	1	280	7.0	20	1400
Stuffed Cabbage	1	210	9.0	40	830
Zucchini Lasagna	1	260	7.0	20	1050
KRAFT					
Macaroni & Cheese	3/4 cup	290	13.0	5	530
Spiral Mac. & Cheese	3/4 cup	330	17.0	10	560
Egg Noodles & Cheese	3/4 cup	340	17.0	50	630
Egg Noodles & Chicken	3/4 cup	240	9.0	35	880
Spaghetti Dinner	1 cup	310	8.0	5	730
Spaghetti Dinner Meat Sauce	1 cup	370	14.0	15	720
Velveeta Shells & Cheese	1/2 cup	260	10.0	25	720
HEALTHY CHOICE					
Chicken Parmigiana	1	290	5.0	65	320
Chicken & Pasta Divan	1	310	4.0	60	560
Chicken Oriental	1	210	1.0	45	410
Sweet & Sour Chicken	1	260	2.0	50	260
Shrimp Creole	1	230	3.0	90	420
Sirloin Tips	1	280	6.0	55	320
Sole au Gratin	1	280	5.0	40	490
Oriental Pepper Steak	1	270	5.0	70	530
Salisbury Steak	1	300	7.0	50	560
Breast of Turkey	1	270	5.0	55	450

CONDIMENTS

Mayonnaise	1 tbsp.	100	11.0	5	80

FOOD	SERVING SIZE	CALORIES	FAT (grams)	CHOLESTEROL (mgs)	SODIUM (mgs)
Tartar sauce	1 tbsp.	95	10.0	10	141
White sauce	2 tbsp.	54	4.1	4	125
Diet mayo.	1 tbsp.	45	5.0	5	90
Imitation mayo.	1 tbsp.	60	4.0	10	100
Miracle Whip	1 tbsp.	70	7.0	5	85
Kraft sandwich spread	1 tbsp.	50	5.0	5	75

DAIRY FOODS

FOOD	SERVING SIZE	CALORIES	FAT	CHOLESTEROL	SODIUM
Whole milk	1 cup	150	8.1	34	120
Low-fat milk	1 cup	122	4.7	20	122
Skim milk	1 cup	89	0.4	5	128
Nonfat dry	1 cup	81	0.2	4	124
Canned evaporated skim	1 oz.	23	trace	1	35
Buttermilk (skim)	1 cup	88	0.2	10	318
Goat milk	1 cup	163	9.8	27	83
Yogurt (nonfat)	1 cup	127	0.4	4	174
Yogurt (low-fat)	1 cup	143	3.4	14	159
Yogurt (whole-milk)	1 cup	141	7.7	30	107
Half & half	1 tbsp.	20	1.7	6	6
Light cream	1 tbsp.	29	2.9	10	6
Medium cream	1 tbsp.	37	3.8	13	6
Light whipped cream	1 tbsp.	44	4.6	17	5
Heavy whipped cream	1 tbsp.	52	5.6	20	6
Sour cream	1 tbsp.	26	2.5	5	6
Formagg sour cream	1 oz.	40	3.0	0	10
Aerosol whipped-cream topping	3/4 cup	25	2.0	10	10

DESSERTS

FOOD	SERVING SIZE	CALORIES	FAT	CHOLESTEROL	SODIUM
Cinnamon roll	1 avg.	174	5.0	39	214
Brownie	1 avg.	146	9.4	25	75
Angel-food cake	2 oz.	161	0.1	0	170
Carrot cake	3 1/2 oz.	356	20.4	30	246
Devil's-food cake	3 oz.	323	15.0	37	357
Gingerbread	2 oz.	175	4.3	0.6	190
Formagg Cheesecake	2 oz.	130	6.0	0	25
Marble cake	3 oz.	288	7.6	40	225
Choco.-chip cookies	1 avg.	52	2.3	6	44
Ladyfingers	1 large	50	1.1	50	10
McDonald's cookies	1 box	292	10.5	9	328
Oatmeal cookies	1 avg.	63	2.2	7	23
Peanut-butter cookies	1 avg.	57	2.3	7	21

FOOD	SERVING SIZE	CALORIES	FAT (grams)	CHOLESTEROL (mgs)	SODIUM (mgs)
Hostess Devil's Food Cupcakes	1	185	6.0	5	282
Hostess Ding Dongs	1	187	10.5	10	121
Hostess Ho Hos	1	118	6.0	14	63
Hostess Suzy Qs	1	256	10.9	10	301
Hostess Twinkies	1	152	6.2	20	203
Custard mixes	1/2 cup	143	4.6	19–24	125+
Doughnuts	1 avg.	125+	6–12	8–100+	75+
Ice cream					
16% fat	1 cup	349	23.8	84	108
10% fat	1 cup	257	14.1	53	116
sandwich	1	238	8.5	34	100+
Eskimo Pie	1	270	19.1	35	100+
Ice milk	1 cup	222	4.6	13	163
Frozen yogurt	1 cup	244	3.0	10	121
Tofu dessert	1 cup	130	10.8	0	95
Sherbet	1 cup	268	4.0	7	92
Pies:					
Hostess Apple	3 1/2 oz.	331	18.1	35	320
Hostess Cherry	3 1/2 oz.	352	17.1	10	180
Sara Lee Bavarian Cream	3 1/2 oz.	352	25.1	23	80
Morton Coconut Custard	3 1/2 oz.	290	15.0	60	150
Lemon meringue	3 1/2 oz.	227	7.5	93	282
Morton peach	3 1/2 oz.	260	12.0	10	230
Morton Pumpkin	3 1/2 oz.	210	8.0	40	270
Puddings:					
Canned tapioca	3 1/2 oz.	129	3.1	53	185
Vanilla (whole-milk)	3 1/2 oz.	175	4.1	16	251
Vanilla (skim-milk)	1/2 cup	147	0.3	3	258

DIPS

FOOD	SERVING SIZE	CALORIES	FAT (grams)	CHOLESTEROL (mgs)	SODIUM (mgs)
Kraft Premium (various types)	1 oz.	50	4.0	10-20	150+
Guacomole	2 tbsp.	50	4.0	0	210
Buttermilk	2 tbsp.	70	6.0	0	240
French onion	2 tbsp.	60	4.0	0	260
Green onion	2 tbsp.	60	4.0	0	170
Bacon-horseradish	2 tbsp.	60	5.0	0	200
Clam	2 tbsp.	60	5.0	0	250
Garlic	2 tbsp.	60	4.0	0	160

FOOD	SERVING SIZE	CALORIES	FAT (grams)	CHOLESTEROL (mgs)	SODIUM (mgs)
EGGS & SUBSTITUTES					
Whole egg	1 med.	78	5.5	250	59
Egg yolk	1 med.	59	5.2	250	12
Egg white	1 med.	16	trace	0	47
Eggnog	1 cup	352	19.0	149	138
Egg Beaters	1/2 cup	25	0	0	80
Eggstra	1/2 cup	30	0.8	23	56
Eggtime	1/2 cup	40	1.0	0	120
Lucern	1/2 cup	50	2.0	trace	NA
Second Nature	1/2 cup	35	1.6	0	79
Scramblers	1/2 cup	60	3.0	0	150
FAST FOODS					
McDonald's:					
Big Mac	1	541	31.4	75	963
Egg McMuffin	1	352	20.0	191	911
Fish fillet	1	402	22.7	43	707
French fries	1 serv.	211	10.6	14	112
Hamburger	1	257	9.4	26	525
Hamburger with cheese	1	306	13.3	41	724
Apple pie	1	295	18.3	14	408
Quarter Pounder	1	418	20.5	69	278
Quarter Pounder with cheese	1	518	28.6	95	1206
Vanilla shake	1	324	7.8	29	250
Kentucky Fried Chicken:					
Original recipe chicken	3 1/2 oz.	290	17.8	133	535
Extra-crispy chicken	3 1/2 oz.	323	20.8	116	446
Cole slaw	1 serv.	110	5.9	4	237
Mashed potatoes w/ gravy	1 serv.	74	2.0	3	353
Dinner roll	1	52	1.1	trace	83
FATS & OILS					
Bacon fat	1 tbsp.	126	14.0	11	150+
Beef suet	1 tbsp.	216	23.3	21	18
Chicken fat	1 tbsp.	126	14.0	9	0
Lard	1 tbsp.	126	14.0	13	0
Vegetable oil	1 tbsp.	120	13.5	0	0

FOOD	SERVING SIZE	CALORIES	FAT (grams)	CHOLESTEROL (mgs)	SODIUM (mgs)
Butter	1 tbsp.	108	12.0	36	124
Margarine	1 tbsp.	108	12.0	0	Variable
Butter Buds	1 oz.	12	0	0	NA

FISH & SHELLFISH

FOOD	SERVING SIZE	CALORIES	FAT (grams)	CHOLESTEROL (mgs)	SODIUM (mgs)
Caviar (sturgeon)	1 tsp.	26	1.5	25	220
Clams (canned)	1/2 cup	52	0.7	80	36
Clams (raw)	3 1/2 oz.	82	1.9	50	36
Cod (raw)	3 1/2 oz.	78	0.3	50	70
Crab (king)	3 1/2 oz.	93	1.9	60	Variable
Fish sticks (frozen)	3 1/2 oz.	176	8.9	70	180
Flat Fish	3 1/2 oz.	79	0.8	61	78
Haddock	3 1/2 oz.	141	6.6	60	71
Halibut	3 1/2 oz.	214	8.8	60	168
Herring	3 1/2 oz.	176	11.3	85	74
Lobster	3 1/2 oz.	91	1.9	100	210
Mackerel	3 1/2 oz.	191	12.2	95	148
Oysters	3 1/2 oz.	66	1.8	50	73
Salmon	3 1/2 oz.	182	7.4	47	50
Salmon (canned chinook)	3 1/2 oz.	210	14.0	60	300+
Sardines (canned in oil)	3 1/2 oz.	311	24.4	120	510
Scallops	3 1/2 oz.	81	0.2	35	255
Shrimp	3 1/2 oz.	91	0.8	100	140
Trout (brook)	3 1/2 oz.	101	2.1	55	50
Trout (rainbow)	3 1/2 oz.	195	11.4	55	50
Tuna (raw)	3 1/2 oz.	133	3.0	60	37
Tuna (canned in oil)	3 1/2 oz.	197	8.2	63	800+
Tuna (canned in water)	3 1/2 oz.	127	0.8	63	41

GRAIN PRODUCTS

Breads:

FOOD	SERVING SIZE	CALORIES	FAT (grams)	CHOLESTEROL (mgs)	SODIUM (mgs)
Cracked-wheat	1 slice	66	0.6	0	132
English muffin	1 slice	133	1.0	0	203
French	1 slice	75	0.5	0	140
Oatmeal Goodness	1 slice	90	2.0	0	140
Oatmeal Goodness White Oatmeal	1 slice	80	1.0	0	140
Pita (pocket)	1 slice	145	1.0	0	86
Pumpernickel	1 slice	79	0.4	0	182
Raisin	1 slice	66	0.7	0	91

FOOD	SERVING SIZE	CALORIES	FAT (grams)	CHOLESTEROL (mgs)	SODIUM (mgs)
Rye	1 slice	61	0.3	0	139
White	1 slice	68	0.8	0	127
Whole-wheat	1 slice	61	0.8	0	132
Crackers:					
Matzo	1	118	0.3	0	10
Melba toast	3	60	2.0	0.6	2
Saltines	4	48	1.3	1.0	123
Egg noodles	1 cup	200	2.4	50	3
Oatmeal Goodness Muffins	1	140	2.0	0	160
Pancake mix	1 avg.	367	5.0	33	1192
Stuffing mix	1/2 cup	198	8.0	45	515

MEATS

FOOD	SERVING SIZE	CALORIES	FAT (grams)	CHOLESTEROL (mgs)	SODIUM (mgs)
Beef: Cooked, well-trimmed Composite	3 oz.	192	9.4	73	57
Eye round steak	3 oz.	158	6.0	59	52
Top round steak	3 oz.	166	5.9	72	52
Tip roast	3 oz.	167	7.0	69	55
Bottom round	3 oz.	201	9.3	81	44
Sirloin steak	3 oz.	185	8.3	75	56
Top sirloin	3 oz.	182	8.7	65	57
Rib steak	3 oz.	200	10.9	68	58
DAKOTA LEAN					
Chuck	3 oz.	120	5.7	43.3	NA
Ground beef	3 oz.	121	5.2	37.5	NA
N.Y. Strip	3 oz.	101	1.35	34.5	NA
Ribeye	3 oz.	112	1.9	31.2	NA
Sirloin	3 oz.	110	4.15	NA	NA
Rib roast	3 oz.	217	12.9	68	62
Lade pot roast	3 oz.	241	14.3	90	60
Arm pot roast	3 oz.	205	9.3	85	56
Brisket	3 oz.	230	14.3	77	66
Tenderloin	3 oz.	183	8.9	72	54
Ground beef (27% fat)	3 oz.	251	16.9	86	71
Ground beef (18% fat)	3 oz.	233	14.4	86	69
Lamb Composite, cooked, trimmed	3 oz.	176	8.1	78	71
Lamb shank	3 oz.	156	6.0	81	54
Lamb loin chop	3 oz.	188	8.9	82	71
Lamb blade chop	3 oz.	195	10.9	82	80
Lamb rib roast	3 oz.	211	12.9	78	67

FOOD	SERVING SIZE	CALORIES	FAT (grams)	CHOLESTEROL (mgs)	SODIUM (mgs)
Pork composite, cooked, trimmed	3 oz.	198	11.1	79	50
Leg roast	3 oz.	187	9.4	80	55
Top loin chop	3 oz.	219	12.7	80	57
Top loin roast	3 oz.	208	11.7	67	39
Shoulder blade	3 oz.	250	15.0	99	64
Spareribs	3 oz.	338	25.8	103	79
Center loin chop	3 oz.	196	8.9	83	66
Tenderloin	3 oz.	141	4.1	79	57
Sirloin roast	3 oz.	221	11.1	94	50
Center rib chop	3 oz.	219	12.7	80	57
Center rib roast	3 oz.	208	11.7	67	39
Bacon	1 slice	40	3.0	5	120
Ham (3% fat)	3 oz.	120	6.0	45	240
Chicken:					
Light, no skin	3 oz.	153	4.2	66	54
Dark, no skin	3 oz.	156	5.4	78	72
Dark & White, with skin	3 oz.	210	12.6	75	66
Chicken gizzard	1 cup	215	4.8	283	83
Chicken liver	1 cup	200	5.0	800	68
Turkey:					
Light, no skin	3 oz.	153	4.2	66	54
Dark, no skin	3 oz.	156	5.4	78	72
Light & Dark, with skin	3 oz.	210	12.6	75	66
Bologna, franks	1 oz.	71	5.4	37	336
Ham	1 oz.	40	1.5	28	280
Pastrami	1 oz.	34	1.6	29	525
Salami	1 oz.	50	3.5	26	454
Veal:					
Lean only (leg, loin, cutlet)	3 oz.	120	2.7	84	48
Lean & fat (most cuts)	3 oz.	183	9.0	84	39
Lean & fat (rib, breast)	3 oz.	267	23.1	87	42
Duck:					
Flesh only	3 oz.	141	6.9	62	63
Flesh & skin	3 oz.	276	24.3	60	63
Goose:					
Flesh only	3 oz.	135	6.0	63	72
Organ meats:					
Beef kidney	3 1/2 oz.	252	12.0	375	253

FOOD	SERVING SIZE	CALORIES	FAT (grams)	CHOLESTEROL (mgs)	SODIUM (mgs)
Beef liver	3 1/2 oz.	140	4.7	300	73
Chicken liver	3 1/2 oz.	165	4.4	746	61
Beef tongue	3 1/2 oz.	244	16.7	140	61
Beef heart	3 1/2 oz.	179	5.7	274	104
Brains	3 1/2 oz.	106	7.3	2100	106
Sweetbreads	3 1/2 oz.	90	6.6	132	99
Luncheon meats: (Oscar Meyer)					
Bologna	1 oz.	88	8.1	15+	292
Canadian bacon	1 oz.	45	2.0	13	384
Chopped ham	1 oz.	64	4.8	14	387
Ham & cheese loaf	1 oz.	70	5.6		372
Headcheese	1 oz.	55	4.1	28	
Honey loaf	1 oz.	39	1.7	8	377
Liverwurst	1 oz	139	9.1	35	81
Olive loaf	1 oz.	64	4.5	10	416
Salami (dry)	1 oz.	112	9.8	22	540
Spam (Hormel)	1 oz.	87	7.4	15	336
Hot dog	1.6 oz.	142	3.5	23	464
Ham	3 1/2 oz.	120	5.0	50	1527
SALAD DRESSINGS					
Blue cheese	1 tbsp.	71	7.3	4-10	153
Green goddess	1 tbsp.	68	7.0	1	150
Russian	1 tbsp.	74	7.6	7-10	130
Thousand Island	1 tbsp.	70	7.0	9	98
French	1 tbsp.	66	6.2	0	219
Italian	1 tbsp.	83	9.0	0	314

Desirable Weights for Men and Women

HEIGHT (WITH SHOES)	WEIGHT (IN INDOOR CLOTHING)		
	SMALL FRAME	MEDIUM FRAME	LARGE FRAME
MEN			
5 ft. 2 in.	112–120 lbs.	118–129 lbs.	126–141 lbs.
5 ft. 3 in.	115–123 lbs.	121–133 lbs.	129–144 lbs.
5 ft. 4 in.	118–126 lbs.	124–136 lbs.	132–148 lbs.
5 ft. 5 in.	121–129 lbs.	127–139 lbs.	135–152 lbs.
5 ft. 6 in.	124–133 lbs.	130–143 lbs.	138–156 lbs.
5 ft. 7 in.	128–137 lbs.	134–147 lbs.	142–161 lbs.
5 ft. 8 in.	132–141 lbs.	138–152 lbs.	147–166 lbs.
5 ft. 9 in.	136–145 lbs.	142–156 lbs.	151–170 lbs.
5 ft. 10 in.	140–150 lbs.	146–160 lbs.	155–174 lbs.
5 ft. 11 in.	144–154 lbs.	150–165 lbs.	159–179 lbs.
6 ft. 0 in.	148–158 lbs.	154–170 lbs.	164–184 lbs.
6 ft. 1 in.	152–162 lbs.	158–175 lbs.	168–189 lbs.
6 ft. 2 in.	156–167 lbs.	162–180 lbs.	173–194 lbs.
6 ft. 3 in.	160–171 lbs.	167–185 lbs.	178–199 lbs.
6 ft. 4 in.	164–175 lbs.	172–190 lbs.	182–204 lbs.
WOMEN			
4 ft. 10 in.	92– 98 lbs.	96–107 lbs.	104–119 lbs.
4 ft. 11 in.	94–101 lbs.	98–110 lbs.	106–122 lbs.
5 ft. 0 in.	96–104 lbs.	101–113 lbs.	109–125 lbs.
5 ft. 1 in.	99–107 lbs.	104–116 lbs.	112–128 lbs.
5 ft. 2 in.	102–110 lbs.	107–119 lbs.	115–131 lbs.
5 ft. 3 in.	105–113 lbs.	110–122 lbs.	118–134 lbs.
5 ft. 4 in.	108–116 lbs.	113–126 lbs.	121–138 lbs.
5 ft. 5 in.	111–119 lbs.	116–130 lbs.	125–142 lbs.
5 ft. 6 in.	114–123 lbs.	120–135 lbs.	129–146 lbs.
5 ft. 7 in.	118–127 lbs.	124–139 lbs.	133–150 lbs.
5 ft. 8 in.	122–131 lbs.	128–143 lbs.	137–154 lbs.
5 ft. 9 in.	126–135 lbs.	132–147 lbs.	141–158 lbs.
5 ft. 10 in.	130–140 lbs.	136–151 lbs.	145–163 lbs.
5 ft. 11 in.	134–144 lbs.	140–155 lbs.	149–168 lbs.
6 ft. 0 in.	138–148 lbs.	144–159 lbs.	153–173 lbs.

SOURCE: Prepared by the Metropolitan Life Insurance Company. Derived primarily from data of the *Build and Blood Pressure Study*, 1959, Society of Actuaries.

Fiber Content of Various Foods

FOOD	TOTAL DIETARY FIBER*	SOLUBLE FIBER*
GRAINS		
Barley, pearled	10.8	2.8
Cornmeal, wholegrain	15.3	9.0
Oat bran, uncooked	18.6	7.2
Oatmeal, uncooked	12.1	4.9
Rice, brown, dry	7.2	0.7
Rice bran	35.0	33.0
(Vita-Fiber brand Rice Bran)		
FRUITS		
Apple, raw	2.0	0.6
Apple fiber	42.9	11.1
(Tastee Apple brand)		
Prunes, dried	16.1	4.6
Raisins	6.8	1.7
DRIED BEANS & PEAS		
Beans, kidney, canned	6.2	2.7
Beans, kidney, raw	19.9	8.5
Beans, pinto, raw	18.7	7.0
Beans, white, raw	16.2	4.7
Lentils, raw	16.9	3.8
Peas, black-eyed, raw	25.0	11.0
Peas, chick, raw	15.0	7.6
Peas, split, raw	11.9	4.0

*Grams per 100 gram serving (3.5 ounces). Taken from *Plant Fiber in Foods* by James W. Anderson, M.D., with permission from the Nutrition Research Foundation Box 22124 Lexington, KY 40522.

The Shopping List

The following is a list of a few manufacturers of products which I have used and am happy to recommend to you. Since many of these products are not yet widely available in supermarkets, but truly are worth the time and expense of tracking them down, I have listed phone numbers. If you can't find the products in stores, go ahead and call the manufacturer. In some cases they can tell you where the product is carried locally, while in others they can ship their products directly to you.

BRAE BEEF markets low-fat meat, though it is rather expensive. Located in Stamford, CT, call (203) 323-4482, or (800) 323-4484 from out-of-state.

DAKOTA LEAN MEATS sells a whole line of very low-fat beef, truly superior tasting meat. 736 Tripp Avenue, Winner, South Dakota, 57580, or (605) 842-3664. (800) 727-5326.

GALAXY CHEESE makes an entire line of delicious cheese alternatives that are 100% cholesterol and lactose free, very low in saturated fat, and rich sources of monosaturated fat. The products are marketed under the name Formagg. (800) 441-9419.

HEALTH VALLEY FOODS makes a whole line of delicious oat-bran products. 700 Union Street, Montebello, CA 90640, or (213) 724-2211. (800) 423-4846.

JODY'S MUFFIN CO. supplies muffin mixes for both oat bran and rice bran muffins for mail order. (800) 642-1144.

KOLLN makes great-tasting cereals, Oat Bran Crunch and Fruit' n Oat Bran Crunch, which provide substantial amounts of oat bran—making them some of the best ready-to-eat cereals available. (201) 964-8176.

NO YOLKS are a cholesterol-free egg noodle. Foulds, Inc., 520 E. Church Street, Libertyville, IL 60048, or (312) 362-3062.

QUAKER OATS has introduced a ready-to-eat oat bran cereal that is the first on the market to equal the benefits of the original, pure oat bran. Look for the red box labeled Quaker Oat Bran: High Fiber Oat Cereal. One ounce has 20 grams of oat bran, and 4.7 grams of soluble fiber—even more than the 4.2 grams you find in pure oat bran.

SKINNY HAVEN makes a variety of low-fat salad dressings in single-serving packets, to take anywhere. Anaheim, CA, 92805, or (714) 632-8020.

SPICE 'N' SLICE offers packs of spices and herbs that you can mix with freshly ground turkey breast to make your own sausage, salami, bologna, pepperoni, and jerky, without all the fat. Seagull Family Products, Inc., 2231 West Shangri La Road, Suite "T," P.O. Box 26051, Phoenix, Arizona, 85068. (602) 861-4094.

SWEET DECEIT makes delicious, though expensive, fancy cakes that are low in fat. 11444 W. Olympic Blvd., Los Angeles, CA, 90064. (213) 473-6052.

TASTEE APPLE FIBER is another source of soluble fiber that makes a great alternative to oat bran in muffins, cookies, and other baked goods. Look for it in health food stores and supermarkets.

YOWHIP is a delicious whipped topping to put on desserts, with only 1 gram of fat per serving. Toluca Lake, CA, 91602.